# VETERAN PREFERENCE EMPLOYMENT STATUTES

# VETERAN PREFERENCE EMPLOYMENT STATUTES

## A 2ND EDITION

# V. I. BROWN

**VETERAN PREFERENCE EMPLOYMENT STATUTES**
**A 2ND EDITION**

*iUniverse books may be ordered through booksellers or by contacting:*

*iUniverse*
*1663 Liberty Drive*
*Bloomington, IN 47403*
*www.iuniverse.com*
*844-349-9409*

*Because of the dynamic nature of the Internet, any web addresses or links contained in this book may have changed since publication and may no longer be valid. The views expressed in this work are solely those of the author and do not necessarily reflect the views of the publisher, and the publisher hereby disclaims any responsibility for them.*

*Any people depicted in stock imagery provided by Getty Images are models, and such images are being used for illustrative purposes only.*
*Certain stock imagery © Getty Images.*

*ISBN: 978-1-6632-3082-9 (sc)*
*ISBN: 978-1-6632-3083-6 (e)*

*Print information available on the last page.*

*iUniverse rev. date: 01/28/2022*

To the Spirit of Abraham Lincoln, sixteenth President and
Commander-In-Chief of
The Armed Forces of The United States.
He preserved our Union.

# DISCLAIMER

The purpose of this book, Veteran Preference Employment Statues, is to provide information about laws which pertain to veterans. Included herein are excerpts from the actual texts of some of such laws. Further, this work should be examined with the understanding that no legal advice of any kind is presented or implied herein. The author is not an attorney. He is accordingly not qualified to render legal advice. The author who is also publisher assumes no liability for the use, misuse or misinterpretation of the information contained herein.

Only the most pertinent parts of the laws in question are included. Readers interested in the full text of these laws should secure the entire statute from a law library. Legal citations are included herein in order to aid the reader in this respect.

The information herein is accurate as of the date on which this book went to press, based on the sources then available to the author. Some laws may have changed between the time when these statutes were promulgated by the sources responsible and the date of publication of this book. This work should be examined with the understanding that all laws change over time. The author/publisher assumes no responsibility for changes to laws which may have occurred since the statutes in question were promulgated, before or after publication.

# CONTENTS

# INTRODUCTION

*"With malice towards none, with charity for*
*all, with firmness in the right, as*
*God gives us to see the right, let us strive on to finish*
*the work we are in, to bind up the nation's wounds,*
*to care for him who shall have borne the battle,*
*and for his widow and his orphan, to do all*
*which may achieve and cherish*
*a just and lasting peace among ourselves, and with all nations."*

Abraham Lincoln
Second Inaugural Address
President and
Commander-In-Chief
Of The Armed Forces Of
The United States, 1861 - 65
4 March 1865

Upon the occasion of his Second Inauguration, Abraham Lincoln spoke of the need to care for war veterans and their families. It was not the first time a government official had addressed the importance of equitable treatment for this nation's war veterans. However, Lincoln's Second Inaugural Address is generally recognized as the most prominent official commitment to that principle. The government's commitment to veterans and their families continues to this day – and yet it has been the subject of debate since the times of President Lincoln.

The continuing debate could have been observed in the news media as they have reported the efforts within certain circles to modify veterans' benefits. These efforts are evident both in the area of employment and elsewhere. Often the debate has centered on veterans' preference within the Federal Government in reduction-in-force situations (RIFs). Since the publication of the 1st Edition this book, the author is unaware of any erosion of veterans' employment retention rights at the Federal or state level. The media have reported that every effort to erode such rights has been consistently rebuffed. (For a better comprehension of retention rights among the several states and within the Federal Government, see "Retention Preference" in the chapter entitled "Overview of Federal and State Statutes.")

Further, the media have reported that responsible officials have advocated strengthening existing benefits. The overall degree of these officials' success in securing increased benefits is itself open to debate, however. After examining the information herein, the reader may want to monitor the situation through the available media.

The Government has been ably assisted in its efforts to expand and preserve the benefits in question. Influential private interests have consistently taken the initiative in this respect. Possibly the most prominent of these interests is the American Legion (which rendered valuable advice to the author in compiling this book). Witness the efforts of that august body to advocate and to advise legislators to enact the Veterans Employment Opportunities Act Of 1998. On 31 October 1998 President William Jefferson Clinton signed this Act into law. Veterans can therefore take heart, knowing that influential persons have worked and continue to work to preserve their interests.

The American Legion (AL) deserves special mention because of its history of involvement with veterans' issues. Such involvement pertains not merely to the close relationship with the Government which was demonstrated in the enactment of the aforementioned legislation. Without the AL it is possible that many of the laws detailed in this book would not have been enacted.

With the anticipated triumph of the U. S. and its allies during the waning days of the Second World War, the AL set about to ensure that returning veterans would receive official recognition for their sacrifices and military service. These activities were borne of the realization that veterans would need substantial help from the Government in order to readjust to civilian life from their military endeavors. The statutes which were therefore proposed by the AL to achieve this end were realized on 22 June 1944 when the Servicemen's Readjustment Act Of 1944, commonly known as the "G. I. Bill Of Rights" or more succinctly as the "G. I. Bill", was signed into law by President Franklin D. Roosevelt. The District Of Columbia and each of the states eventually enacted similar legislation. The foundation which the AL laid to help facilitate veterans' readjustment remains in place to this day. (For a detailed chronicle of the AL and its activities to secure benefits and official recognition for veterans, see *The American Legion: An Official History 1919 – 1989* by Thomas A. Rumer [M. Evans & Co., Inc., 1990].)

Not long after the 1st Edition of this book was completed, The Washington *Post* published an article entitled "Expanded Benefits For Veterans" (15 January 1999, p. A. 27). Soon after, the same paper published "The Tale Of The Aging Mariners" (19 January 1999, p. A.17). That article detailed the apparent lack of recognition of persons who served in the Merchant Marine during WWII, despite their contribution – which helped win that war – and the hardships they faced. This book will demonstrate that some states have taken the initiative and prescribed in their statutes that Merchant Mariners receive the same consideration as other veterans.

The aforementioned debate continues. One can safely wager that the intensity of this debate will not subside subsequent to the publication of this book. Accordingly, each veteran should take responsibility to monitor the debate over the laws pertaining to his or her own situation.

Veterans should also realize that more needs to be done. The forces that seek to erode veterans' benefits are quite strong, and indications are that these forces are exerting increasing influence over the debate. It is therefore the author's fervent hope that the information contained herein will induce veterans and their families to become more involved in the debate in order to protect their own interests. The author expects that the information contained herein will aid in the debate at both the federal and state levels.

It is worth noting however, that for some reason which this author has yet to determine, the debate concerning veterans' benefits has appeared to center almost exclusively around benefits at the Federal level. This author is not aware of any debate concerning the benefits which each state affords honorably discharged veterans. Accordingly, this author solicits information concerning any such debate at the state level.

This book will concentrate on state statutes. There are good reasons for this focus. One is that persons departing the military will almost always be returned to their home of record where they should be more concerned with local (state) statutes. Further, with respect to the equitable treatment of war veterans, as proclaimed by Commander-In-Chief Lincoln, as the Federal Government goes then so go the states. To reiterate, every state in the Union, as well as the District Of Columbia, has enacted laws to ensure that those who have borne arms in the defense of freedom and liberty will receive proper compensation and consideration in government employment.

Accordingly, the purpose of this book is to provide a centralized source to inform honorably discharged veterans of the laws which the several states and the U. S. Government and the District Of Columbia have enacted in their behalf. Veterans will find a number of uses for the information herein. The author offers the following suggestions in this regard.

# SUGGESTED USES FOR THIS BOOK

## EDUCATION AND INFORMATION

With this book, veterans can educate or inform themselves as to the extent to which the government has committed itself to ensuring their equitable treatment. Further, they can become aware of the vast array and complexity of the laws on the subject of employment preferences for veterans.

Some states have included language explicitly expressing their gratitude for the sacrifices veterans have made and continue to make for this nation. For a detailed discussion of these states and their respective statutes, refer to the chapter entitled "Special Mention." Veterans will be pleased, as well as enlightened, by the appreciation which the government has shown.

## EMPLOYMENT CHOICES

Veterans can use this book in order to make informed decisions about their careers. It might indeed be advantageous for one who has been honorably discharged from the military to pursue a government career. A veteran might want to make this career choice not only because governments are required to prefer them for employment. It is worth considering the security that is normally a part of government service as opposed to private sector employment.

Some states also prefer to retain veterans who are on the payroll when they cut their labor forces during reductions-in-force. Here the author is compelled to offer the benefit of his own experience on the subject of government reductions-in-force. While he was employed with the State Of California, the state cut its workforce at a certain agency by 3,500 in one month. Those veterans who were on the payroll at the time must certainly have been grateful for any retention rights giving them preference over non-veterans. (The author was not employed at the agency which experienced the cut. He was therefore not affected).

In conjunction with the above, the author is further compelled to offer his own experience with the issue of government employment preference. After having been honorably discharged from the U. S. Navy, he was examined for employment with the states of California, Missouri, Pennsylvania and with the U. S. Government. After having been so examined, all four governments were required by statute to afford the author numerical preference of (10), (5), (5) and (5), respectively. The author did indeed subsequently secure employment with all four of said governments. It is not likely that the author would have been hired with any of the aforementioned governments if he had not been afforded veterans' preference.

The subject of retention rights will be addressed later in this book. The point here is that governments sometimes do cut their labor forces. Accordingly, retention rights can be a very valuable commodity.

The laws which follow later in this book specify benefits in addition to the retention preference referred to above. For example, sometimes veteran's preference is applicable to those who seek better-paying jobs after initial entry into the civil service.

## LOCATION AFTER DISCHARGE

Honorably discharged veterans would do well to secure a copy of this book prior to discharge. The information herein can be useful in making a decision on where to settle. In this regard, the statutes detailed herein will provide fine details concerning residency requirements which some states have for veterans who apply for employment preference.

Further, the statutes detailed herein allow the veteran to compare the relative benefits among the states. These benefits vary widely. Should a veteran consider public employment, then it might be advantageous to settle in one state as opposed to another.

Here again the author is compelled to offer the benefit of his experience in this area. While he was employed with the State Of Missouri he was also examined for employment with a neighboring state, Kansas. He traveled to Kansas for the examination. Kansas authorities did award the author the preference required by the applicable Kansas statute which was added to his earned passing score. While he was still a resident of Missouri he was subsequently contacted by Kansas authorities when a position came open. Kansas is one state which did not have, as of the publication of the 1st Edition of this book, a residency requirement. (The author opted instead for more lucrative employment with the U. S. Government in Washington, DC).

## RELOCATION

Using this book as a guide, a veteran already settled in one area may decide to relocate to another state where benefits are more generous. In this regard, veterans should realize that relocation does not necessarily entail a long-distance move. There are numerous metropolitan areas in the U. S. which overlap state boundaries. Here are but three: (1) St. Louis, MO/East St. Louis, IL, (2) Camden, NJ/Philadelphia, PA, and (3) Portland, OR/Vancouver, WA. A simple move across a river might indeed be advantageous. Such a move might considerably enhance one's prospects for public employment – something to consider, even for a veteran currently working in the private sector. Perhaps that veteran will want to move into public employment at a later date.

Veterans are reminded however, to study the residency requirements already mentioned. They should also keep in mind that some states have limits on the amount of time that a veteran has to apply for employment preference. These limits might be in addition to any residency requirements. A timely relocation to another part of a metropolitan area might therefore be advantageous if a veteran believes that she or he might prefer public employment at some future date.

## SCOPE OF THIS BOOK

The primary purpose of this book is to inform honorably discharged veterans of the laws which afford them preference in employment. This work is the first comprehensive and consolidated listing and analysis of these statutes.

To reiterate, the emphasis here will be on state statutes. However, the Federal statutes on this subject are also included because many of the state statutes are linked to the comparable Federal statutes. In some cases the state statute will specify that honorably discharged veterans will be afforded whatever the comparable Federal statute provides.

Further, it could be said that the state statutes are modeled after comparable statutes of the Federal Government. Therefore, anyone who desires a "feel" for the general language of the state laws need only examine the Federal statutes. Finally, state laws are emphasized here because although the Federal statutes are widely available throughout these United States, the state statutes are not. Accordingly both the Federal and state statutes are included for ready comprehension.

Further, the information herein is expressly not intended for certain purposes. Specifically:

## THIS BOOK DOES NOT PROVIDE INTERPRETATION OF LAWS

The author hereby reiterates the information in the disclaimer at the beginning of this book. The author is not an attorney. Neither is he a member of the bar of any state. He is therefore not qualified to interpret laws for another individual. His intention is merely to provide the text of the laws in question.

All of the pertinent passages of the Federal and state laws which pertain to veterans' employment preferences are included in this book. Any individual is free to interpret these laws as she or he sees fit. Indeed, the reader is encouraged to examine these laws for information and education.

Inasmuch as the author is not an attorney and is not himself perfect, the reader may find something in the law which is pertinent and which the author missed. The reader is advised however, to first review the Quick Reference Guide included in this book. The Guide was created expressly to facilitate the examination and comparison of these statutes.

## THIS BOOK DOES NOT PROVIDE LEGAL ADVICE

This book does not purport to provide legal advice on any matter. No advice concerning the laws in question will be given, nor any advice on how to interpret them, nor any advice on the manner in which an individual should apply for veteran's preference.

## THIS BOOK DOES NOT DETAIL
## PERIPHERAL STATUTES

In addition to the laws detailed in this book, there is another series of Federal and state laws pertaining to veterans. These laws will not be addressed in this book because they are not pertinent to veterans' employment preferences.

Possibly the best example of the aforementioned peripheral statutes are the laws enacted to protect the rights of discharged men and women who seek reinstatement to their previous jobs. These are commonly called "re-employment rights." These laws were enacted to ensure that veterans would be re-employed in the civilian jobs which they left when they either were called to active duty by the Selective Service (draft) or decided voluntarily to participate in a war effort.

Laws which ensure re-employment rights are not the subject of this book for two reasons. First of all, they are now fairly redundant. There are presently negligible numbers of ex-service men and women who seek re-employment into the jobs from which they were conscripted or which they voluntarily departed for military service. No one has been conscripted by the U. S. Government since 1973. Further, the numbers of persons who left their civilian jobs in order to participate in a war effort since the end of the Vietnam Conflict in 1975 is in all likelihood negligible.

Second, the laws which ensure re-employment rights for returning service personnel are always detailed separately from the laws which detail employment preference. The states and the Federal Government are fairly uniform in promulgating laws pertaining to re-employment rights. However, governments are also fairly uniform in promulgating separate statutes which address such matters. For the above two reasons, the author has declined to include such statutes.

## THIS BOOK DOES NOT DETAIL
## PERSONNEL REGULATIONS

The laws which are provided later in this book are not regulations. Neither should these laws be construed as such. The reader should understand that some states (MD, for instance) not only promulgate laws, but also promulgate elaborate personnel regulations which are extensions of the laws. The regulations specify in detail how the law is to be administered.

Some regulations are included in this book in order to make it as informative as possible. Personnel regulations are included under "State Statutes" for those states which declined to specify a precise numerical preference in the comparable law. These regulations are not, however, regarded by the author as vital to the primary purpose of this book. This explains the absence of personnel regulations for most of the states. Should the reader require the applicable regulation which augments the statute in question for a particular state, then he or she should contact the personnel officer for that state.

## **HOW TO USE THIS BOOK**

To derive the maximum benefit from the information in this book, the reader should begin, not with the statutes which make up the first three chapters of the text, but with the Quick Reference Guide which is included later following the section "Special Mention: States With Appreciative Or Notably Beneficial

Statutes." It may seem odd to begin at the back of the book, but there are good reasons for this.

The dry language of the statutes was meant for legal scholars. The author does not expect that most of the persons who secure a copy of this book will be well-versed in how to examine statutes. The statutes are included in order to make the reader aware of what the law requires to be given to veterans. The text of the statutes augments the Quick Reference Guide that follows them. The Guide is a concise summary of, and ready reference to, the entire contents of this book.

Further, the statutes are included in order to ensure that the reader is not swayed by the perceptions of the author. The author is neither an attorney nor a legal expert. Accordingly, the statutes are provided for the reader to compare their information with the data provided in the Quick Reference Guide. The reader is thereby enabled to form her or his own conclusions.

# OVERVIEW OF FEDERAL
# AND STATE STATUTES

The Federal and state statutes which pertain to veterans' preferences have many characteristics in common. As stated before, the states generally appear to have used the Federal Government as a model to write their statutes. This commonality between the Federal and state statutes facilitates their comprehension. If one can comprehend one of the statutes, then the understanding of another, similar statute is that much easier.

Following are the characteristics one can generally observe in laws which pertain to veterans' preference.

## EXAMINATION

All of the statutes, both Federal and state, generally require that a veteran must take and pass a standardized examination in order to be eligible for the preference. The statutes explicitly state that one must have achieved a passing score on the exam before any preference points are added. (A possible exception to this provision is South Dakota, which has rather unique language in its statute). The preference points are added to the earned score in order to arrive at the final score. The final score will determine the veteran's relative ranking on the register or the certificate. It is from these documents that hiring decisions are made. Here the author is compelled to offer his own experience in this regard. On a written examination for the position of Certification Analyst with the State Of California the author achieved an earned score of (83). To this earned score was added ten points, which brought the author's final score to (93). The author was hired because of his final score. Further, most often the examination must be written. Some states do however allow for other types of examinations.

In conjunction with the above, the author is again compelled to offer his own experience with the government hiring process. Some government entities hire without an interview or an oral examination. Only the final score is used for hiring decisions. On the now-defunct P.A.C.E. (Professional And Administrative Career Examination) the author earned a final score of (90). This included five veteran's points. The author was hired based on his final score without an interview. The Federal agency which hired the author sent correspondence to him notifying him that he was hired in Washington, DC. The author was at that time domiciled in Missouri. Lastly, the personnel office which serviced the agency where the author was hired informed him that it was not likely that he would have been hired if the veterans points had not been added to his earned score.

In this book the terms "register" and "certificate are used interchangeably. The register or certificate, or "cert" in Federal personnel jargon, is merely a listing of all of the persons who achieved a passing score on an examination. It is used to prepare the final document from which hiring decisions are made. In Massachusetts the document is referred to as a "requisition." In South Dakota the legal term is "certification."

## PREFERENCE POINTS

Governments usually specify a definite number of points which the veteran will be given upon passing the examination. This number varies from state to state and within the Federal Government, depending on what has been written into the law. In reviewing the texts of the statutes following, the reader will observe that some governments are more generous than others. The reader will also note that governments do not always specify in the law the precise amount of preference. A few states merely specify in the law that preference be given to eligible veterans. This does not necessarily mean that no precise number of preference points will be given, however. This merely means that the law does not specify such. In cases such as this, the states also promulgate elaborate personnel regulations in addition to the law. The regulations will specify the amount of preference. (See "Eligibility Of Kin", below).

Moreover, the number of points which the veteran will receive may depend upon his or her classification. All veterans of course fall into various classifications depending on their military tenure. A "regular" veteran usually receives a minimum of five points. Disabled veterans almost always receive five points more than the "regular" veteran. There are some notable exceptions however, and some states require that all veterans receive the same amount of preference.

In addition, the laws usually allow for the awarding of preference points to the veteran's kin if (1) the veteran is disabled, or (2) the veteran has died while on active duty. It is worth noting that a veteran need not have died as a result of hostilities in order to receive the preference. Any service-related death will qualify the kin to receive the preference. (For more on this subject, see "Eligibility Of Kin", below).

## SPECIFIED PERIOD OF SERVICE

### DURING HOSTILITIES

The individual states and the Federal Government are fairly uniform in specifying which periods of service qualify the veteran to receive the preference. Most often the veteran must have served during a period of hostilities between the U. S. and a foreign power. There are some notable exceptions among the several states, however. These exceptions will be addressed later.

### ACTIVE ENGAGEMENT IN A MILITARY CAMPAIGN

It is important to note that the statutes which are the subject of this book are subject to revision by the respective legislatures. Governments always modify their statutes to reference wars or military campaigns in which this nation has or may become involved. Some states even explicitly provide that the law granting employment preference to veterans will include any hostilities in which the U. S. may subsequently become involved after the statutes in question were enacted.

In view of the above, one should not assume that the statutes in this book are etched in granite. The law may indeed grant preference to veterans who served during periods that are not expressly stated in the law. If there is any question about which periods of service qualify a veteran to receive any preference, then one should contact the cognizant state authorities for an updated interpretation of the law.

## VETERAN DEFINED

### REGULAR VETERAN

Various governments define the term "veteran" differently. Most often the definition is stated explicitly within the text of the law. However, one should further realize that some states devote a separate statute to the definition of the term "veteran." In other states the term is defined by the context of the statute which grants the preference.

To reiterate, a veteran is usually construed to be any person who served in the military during a prescribed period for an interval of at least 180 days. One must always have served for a period other than for training. Reservists who served only for training are thereby usually excluded from receiving any form of preference. However, one state does afford employment preference for persons who served in the National Guard. The Quick Reference Guide which is included later in this book will facilitate the review of the laws on this subject.

## DISABLED VETERAN

**Interpretation**. The definition of a "disabled" veteran is also subject to various interpretations by governments. It is worth noting that the Federal Government does not specify a precise percentage of disability which a veteran must have in order to be declared "disabled", as do some of the states. Within the Federal Government, one need only have been awarded some designation of disability from the U. S. Department Of Veterans Affairs ("V. A.") and also receive some compensation.

**Dept. Of Veterans Affairs Definition.** All of the states defer to the V. A. in matters of disabilities. The states will invariably accept the opinion of the V. A. concerning a veteran's degree of disability. Apparently none of the states have the means to evaluate veterans in this respect. Also invariably, the states will specify in the law that one must have an official designation from the V. A. in order to receive the higher amount of preference for being disabled.

**Percentage of Disability.** Even though all of the states defer to the V. A. in matters of disabilities, some states require that a veteran have a minimum percentage of disability, as declared by the V. A., in order to receive disability preference. Again, this is an area where there is a wide disparity among the several states. The most common percentage by which the veteran must have been disabled in order to receive the higher preference is 10 percent.

Further, the percentage of disability which the veteran has been awarded is sometimes linked to the amount of preference the spouse will receive. One state requires that the veteran must be totally disabled in order for the spouse to receive any preference. It is further worth noting that sometimes the spouse receives the same preference which the disabled veteran would receive. In other states the spouse is only allowed the same number of points which are afforded a "regular" veteran.

## VETERAN DEFINED BY BRANCH OF SERVICE

The Federal Government does not define the term "veteran" in the same manner as do some of the states. The Federal Government includes all branches of the military (Army. Navy, Air Force, Marine Corps & Coast Guard) in its definition. Some states do not. The language of the law in some states fails to mention the Coast Guard. This does not necessarily mean that veterans of the Coast Guard will face exclusion from receiving any form of preference in the states in question. This merely means that the legislature which enacted the statute declined to specifically refer to this service branch. Here is another area where it might behoove one to secure an interpretation of the law in question. The best place to start might be to contact the Personnel Officer of the respective state.

Some states do explicitly include the Coast Guard in their definition of "veteran." There is a reason why the legislature which enacted the law saw fit to do so. The Quick Reference Guide will show those states which include the Coast Guard in their statute.

# ELIGIBILITY OF KIN

The eligibility of the kin of a deceased or a disabled veteran to receive some form of preference is another area where there are many variations among the governments. The states and the Federal Government are fairly uniform in providing some form of preference to a surviving spouse, but some states are more generous than others in this respect.

Some states specify that a deceased veteran's orphans will receive employment preference in addition to his or her surviving spouse. Here also there is great variation, with the states differing on the extent to which other of the veteran's kin can receive some form of preference.

Some states such as New Hampshire (NH) distinguish between unmarried surviving spouses of qualifying veterans and unremarried surviving spouses of qualifying veterans whose death was service-connected. The latter may receive a higher preference.

The Federal statute includes quite explicit and detailed language to address the eligibility of kin. Some states, of which Wisconsin (WI) is possibly the best example, have followed the lead of the Federal Government and prescribed in fine detail which of the veteran's kin will receive preference. Wisconsin is the only state which affords preference to a veteran's divorced wife under certain circumstances.

In view of the above, the statutes on kin eligibility should be read carefully.

# LACK OF SEXIST LANGUAGE

It does bear mentioning that there is a noticeable lack of sexist language in the laws of most of the states and the Federal Government. Governments appear to have made a valiant effort to exclude language which could be labeled as sexist. In reviewing the statutes which follow one can observe few references to the terms "wife" or "husband", for example. These terms have for the most part been replaced by the term "spouse."

There are however some glaring exceptions to the above contention concerning a lack of sexist language. Possibly the best example of such an exception can be observed in the Federal statute 5 U.S.C. (Title 5 of the United States Code) 2108(f) which is included later herein. The aforementioned Wisconsin statute which details providing for divorced wives is another example. However, the law in Wisconsin appears to be justified in using the language in question because of the peculiar circumstances which that law addresses.

The law has changed profoundly since the 1st Edition of this work was promulgated. On 26 June 2015 the Supreme Court declared same sex marriage legal. In the case of *Obergefell v. Hodges,* 409 U. S. 810, the Court ruled that any spouse of any sex can claim, and are entitled by law, to the same benefits as anyone of the opposite sex. Accordingly, each state was thereby obligated to bring its pertinent statute into compliance with the new interpretation of Federal law. (See Federal Statutes, below, under Title 38, U. S. C. Sec 31, Definitions.)

# RETENTION PREFERENCE

It stands to reason that if governments prefer veterans when hiring, then these governments will also want to retain veterans when it is necessary to cut their labor forces.

The states and the Federal Government are fairly uniform in affording veterans some form of preference during reductions-in-force. To reiterate the information which the author previously provided under Suggested Uses For This Book/Employment Choices, sometimes governments do cut their labor forces. There are some restrictions, however. Some states provide that only non-retirees will receive some form of preference. This is another area where there is a wide disparity among the states. The Quick Reference Guide will help the reader compare the statutes from state-to-state.

There has been considerable debate within the Federal Government recently on the subject of veterans' retention preference. The U. S. Government provides that veterans must always be retained before non-veterans during reductions-in-force, irrespective of the veteran's seniority. Persons in some circles have suggested that this form of preference should be restricted or abolished. These efforts to abolish or curtail veterans' retention preference have been unsuccessful so far. One can be assured, however that the debate on this subject will continue.

# ONE-TIME PREFERENCE

The federal and state governments generally hold that any preference which is afforded a veteran will be only upon initial entry into the civil service. Once the preference is used on an open competitive examination in which preference points are added to an earned score, then the preference cannot again be invoked. Within this context, an open competitive examination is one which is used for initial entry into the civil service - not a promotional examination used as a means for advancement within the civil service after initial entry.

Here the federal and state governments are fairly uniform in restricting the preference to initial entry. There are noticeable exceptions, however. Some states expressly provide that a veteran can invoke the preference for the duration of his or her career. One state provides that a veteran can invoke the preference an unlimited number of times in any examination, as long as other state employees are not being considered for the position. There are also special provisions for veterans who have distinguished themselves by having been awarded special military decorations. Refer to the Quick Reference Guide.

# PLACEMENT ON REGISTER

The primary aim of the veterans preference laws is of course to determine veterans' place on the register which determines who will be hired. The states and the federal government are unanimous in requiring that veterans be placed on the register ahead of non-veterans who have the same score. All governments are further uniform in the requirement that disabled veterans be placed ahead of "regular" veterans with the same score. One state requires that disabled veterans be placed at the top of the register, irrespective of their earned score on the examination. Refer to the Quick Reference Guide.

# DISCHARGES

## PREREQUISITE FOR SECURING PREFERENCE

There is one attribute in the federal and state statutes which is a prerequisite for all of the others: a discharge under honorable conditions. The reason for this is simple: Any government would be loathe to employ an individual who had dishonored this republic and its uniform while serving in the military. Accordingly, the states and the Federal Government are uniform in their requirement that one must have served under honorable conditions in order to receive the amount of preference required by law.

One should note however that a discharge under less than honorable conditions might not necessarily preclude an individual from securing public employment. Holding this type of discharge simply means that one may not receive the amount of employment preference specified in the law. Individual states may indeed have laws on their books which preclude persons who received dishonorable discharges, for example, from securing any form of public employment, but this author has not encountered any such provision in his examination of the statutes included herein. This author hereby solicits any information which specifies that persons with discharges under less than honorable conditions are barred from securing public employment.

One governmental entity, the District of Columbia, offers its own unique perspective on this subject. The nation's capital is the only entity which allows for a veteran who was discharged under other than honorable conditions to receive some form of employment preference. The law of the District of Columbia does not specify the precise procedure which must be followed in order for such a person to secure employment preference. This procedure would be detailed in a personnel regulation, which is beyond the scope of this book. The statute is nonetheless on the books, and it is provided later in this volume.

## TYPES OF DISCHARGES

Here is an area where one might encounter some controversy. Only a few states explicitly require that one must have earned an "honorable discharge" in order to receive any form of employment preference. Most states and the federal government merely require that one must have been discharged under honorable conditions. Refer co the Quick Reference Guide for those entities which have this requirement.

Any person who served in the military should have been informed that a general discharge under honorable conditions is not the same as an honorable discharge. It is therefore worth noting that most states and the Federal Government regard these two types of discharges as being equal for the purpose of granting employment preference. Further, the 4,583 persons who were discharged from the army alone in FY 1997 with a general discharge under honorable conditions might be pleased to know this fact. These veterans might be further heartened to know that governments perceive them as equal, for employment purposes, to the 73,107 persons who did receive honorable discharges from the army during the aforementioned period.

The point here is that the explicit provisions in the law for "honorable discharges" as opposed to general discharges under honorable conditions might cause some degree of debate. In this regard, the author is compelled to offer the benefit of his own experience on this subject.

The author is quite familiar with the subject of military discharges. He is a Vietnam Veteran of the U. S. Navy. In that capacity he served in a personnel-related function. One of the first things he recalls learning after having reported for active duty was that an honorable discharge is different from, and superior to, a General Discharge under honorable conditions. Upon being informed of this fact, he resolved to secure an honorable discharge. Failure to do so, he reasoned, would impede his readjustment to civilian life and possibly restrict his employment choices. The author's goal was achieved. He was released from active duty on 10 August 1974 with an honorable discharge.

Moreover, the author has previously been employed as a personnel analyst for a state government and for the U. S. Department of the Treasury. A regular part of his job in these capacities was to review military discharge certificates (Form DD 214) in order to determine the suitability of persons who claimed employment preference based on their military service. In both of these capacities the author was informed that the general policy of the organization was not to distinguish between the two types of discharges in question. Persons who held either type of discharge were regarded as equal for employment purposes.

# FEDERAL STATUTES

The following are the Federal statutes (U. S. Code or "U. S. C.") which pertain to employment preferences for honorably discharged veterans. Inasmuch as there are a myriad of federal statutes which pertain to this subject, only those which are the most pertinent are excerpted here, with only the most pertinent parts provided.

I. **Title 38, U. S. C.**
**Sec. 101. Definitions**

(2)   The term "veteran" means a person who served in the active military, naval, or air service, and who was discharged or released therefrom under conditions other than dishonorable.

(3)   The term "surviving spouse" means (except for purposes of chapter 19 of this title) a person of the opposite sex who was a spouse of a veteran at the time of the veteran's death, and who lived with the veteran continuously from the date of marriage to the date of the veteran's death (except where

there was a separation which was due to the misconduct of, or procured by, the veteran without the fault of the spouse) and who has not remarried or (in cases not involving remarriage) has not since the death of the veteran, and after September 19, 1962, lived with another person and held himself or herself out openly to the public to be the spouse of such other person.

(10) The term "Armed Forces" means the United States Army, Navy, Marine Corps, Air Force, and Coast Guard, including the reserve components thereof.

(11) The term "period of war" means the Spanish-American War, the Mexican border period, World War I, World War II, the Korean conflict, the Vietnam era, the Persian Gulf War, and the period beginning on the date of any future declaration of war by the Congress and ending on the date prescribed by Presidential proclamation or concurrent resolution of the Congress.

(12) The term "veteran of any war" means any veteran who served in the active military, naval, or air service during a period of war.

(29) The term "Vietnam era" means the period beginning August 5, 1964, and ending on May 7, 1975.

(31) The term "spouse" means a person of the opposite sex who is a wife or husband.

(32) The term "former prisoner of war" means a person who, while serving in the active military, naval or air service, was forcibly detained or interned in the line of duty-

    (A) by an enemy government or its agents, or a hostile force, during a period of war; or

    (B) by a foreign government or its agents, or a hostile force, under circumstance which the Secretary finds to have been comparable to the circumstances under which persons have generally been forcibly detained by enemy governments during periods of war.

    (C) The term "Persian Gulf War" means the period beginning on 2 August 1990 and ending on the date thereafter prescribed by Presidential proclamation or by law.

## Sec. 1101. Definitions:

For the purpose of this chapter, the term "veteran" includes a person who died in the active military, naval or air service.

## Sec. 1102. Special provisions relating to surviving spouses

(a)  No compensation shall be paid to the surviving spouse of a veteran under this chapter unless such surviving spouse was married to such veteran-

  (1)  before the expiration of fifteen years after the termination of the period of service in which the injury or disease causing the death of the veteran was incurred or aggravated; or

  (2)  for one year or more; or

  (3)  for any period of time if a child was born of the marriage, or was born to them before the marriage.

## II. Title 5, U. S. C.
## Sec. 2108. Veteran; disabled veteran; preference eligible

For the purpose of this title-

(1)  "veteran" means an individual who-

  (A)  served on active duty in the armed forces during a war, in a campaign or expedition for which a campaign badge has been authorized, or during the period beginning April 28, 1952, and ending July l, 1955; or

  (B)  served on active duty as defined by section 101(21) of title 38 at any time in the armed forces for a period of more than 180 consecutive days any part of which occurred after January 31, 1955, and before the date of the enactment of the Veterans' Education and Employment Assistance Act of 1976, not including service under section 511 (d) of title 10 pursuant to an enlistment in the Army National Guard or the Air National Guard or as a Reserve for service in the Army Reserve, Naval Reserve, Air Force Reserve, Marine Corps Reserve, or Coast Guard Reserve; and who has been separated from the armed forces under honorable conditions;

(2)   "disabled veteran" means an individual who has served on active duty in the armed forces, has been separated therefrom under honorable conditions, and has established the present existence of a service-connected disability or is receiving compensation, disability retirement benefits, or pension because of a public statute administered by the Department of Veterans Affairs or a military department;

(3)   "preference eligible" means, except as provided in paragraph (4) of this section-

(A)   a veteran as defined by paragraph (l)(A) of this section;

(B)   a veteran as defined by paragraph (l)(B) of this section;

(C)   a disabled veteran;

(D)   the unmarried widow or widower of a veteran as defined by paragraph (l)(A) of this section;

(E)   the wife or husband of a service-connected disabled veteran if the veteran has been unable to qualify for any appointment in the civil service or in the government of the District of Columbia;

(F)  the mother of an individual who lost his life under honorable conditions while serving in the armed forces during a period named by paragraph (l)(A) of this section, if

  (i)    her husband is totally and permanently disabled;

  (ii)   she is widowed, divorced or separated from the father and has not remarried; or

  (iii)  she has remarried but is widowed, divorced, or legally separated from her husband when preference is claimed; and

(G)  the mother of a service-connected permanently and totally disabled veteran if-

  (i)    her husband is totally and permanently disabled;

  (ii)   she is widowed, divorced or separated from the father and has not remarried; or

  (iii)  she has remarried but is widowed, divorced or legally separated from her husband when preference is claimed; but does not include applicants for, or members of, the Senior Executive Service, the Defense Intelligence Senior Executive Service, the Senior Cryptologic Executive Service, the Federal Bureau of Investigation and Drug Enforcement Administration Senior Executive Service, or The General Accounting Office;

(4)  except for the purposes of chapters 43 and 75 of this title, "preference eligible" does not include a member of the armed forces unless-

    (A)  the individual is a disabled veteran; or

    (B)  the individual retired below the rank of major or its equivalent; and

(5)  "retired member of the armed forces" means a member or former member of the armed forces who is entitled, under statute, to retired, retirement, or retainer pay on account of service as a member.

## Sec. 3112. Disabled veterans; non-competitive appointment

Under such regulations as the Office of Personnel Management shall prescribe, an agency may make a non-competitive appointment leading to conversion to a career or career-conditional employment of a disabled veteran who has a compensable service-connected disability of 30% or more.

## Sec. 3309. Preference eligible; examinations; additional points for

A preference eligible who receives a passing grade on an examination for entrance into the competitive service is entitled to additional points above his earned rating, as follows:

(1)    a preference eligible under sec. 2108 (3)(C)-(G) of this title-ten points; and

(2)    a preference eligible under sec. 2108 (3)(A) of this title-five points

## Section 3313. Competitive service; registers of eligibles

The names of applicants who have qualified in examinations for the competitive service shall be entered on the appropriate registers or lists of eligibles in the following order-

(1)    for scientific and professional positions in GS-9 or higher, in the order of their ratings, including points added under section 3309 of this title; and

(2)    for all other positions-

    (A)    disabled veterans who have a compensable service-connected disability of ten percent or more, in the order of their ratings, including points added under section 3309 of this title; and

(B)  remaining applicants, in the order of their ratings, including points added under section 3309 of this title.

## Sec. 3501. Definition; application

(a)(3) a preference eligible employee who is a retired member of a uniformed service is considered a preference eligible only if-

(A)  his retirement was based on disability

    (i)  resulting from injury or disease received in the line of duty as a direct result of armed conflict; or

    (ii)  caused by an instrumentality of war and incurred in the line of duty during a period of war defined by sections 101 and 1101 of title 38;

(B)  his service does not include 20 or more years of full-time active service, regardless of when performed, but not including periods of active duty for training.

## Sec. 3502. Order of Retention

(a)  The Office of Personnel Management (OPM) shall prescribe regulations for the release of competing employees in a reduction-in-force which gives due effect to:

(1)  tenure of employment

(2)  military preference, subject to 3501 (a)(3) of this title.

(3)   length of service, and

(4)   efficiency or performance ratings

In computing length of service, a competing employee-

(A)   who is not a retired member of a uniformed service is entitled to credit for the total length of time in active service in the armed forces;

(B)   who is a retired member of a uniformed service is entitled to credit for-

(i)   the length of time in active service in the armed forces during a war, or in a campaign or expedition for which a campaign badge has been authorized; or

(ii)   the total length of time in active service in the armed forces if he is included under section 3501 (a)(3)(A), (B), or (C) of this title; and

(C)   is entitled to credit for-

(i)   service rendered as an employee of a county committee established pursuant to section 8 (b) of the Soil Conservation and Allotment Act or of a committee or association of producers described in section 10 (b) of the Agricultural Adjustment Act; and

(ii)   service rendered as an employee described in section 2105 (c) if such employee moves or has moved, on or after January 1, 1966, without a break in service of more than three days, from a position in a non-apportioned fund instrumentality of the Department of Defense or the Coast Guard to a position in the Department of Defense Or Coast Guard, respectively, that is not described in section 2105 (c).

(b)   A preference eligible described in section 2108 (3)(C) of this title who has a compensable service-connected disability of 30 percent or more and whose performance has not been rated unacceptable under a performance appraisal system implemented under chapter 43 of this title is entitled to be retained in preference to other preference eligibles.

(c)   An employee who is entitled to retention preference and whose performance has not been rated unacceptable under a performance appraisal system implemented under chapter 43 of this title is entitled to be retained in preference to other competing employees.

# STATE STATUTES

The following are the state statutes which pertain to employment preferences for honorably discharged veterans. For the purpose of this book, the District of Columbia is considered to be equal to a state. As is the case with the federal statutes, a myriad of state laws pertain to this subject. Only those state laws which are the most pertinent are excerpted here. Note also that only the most pertinent parts of the excerpted statutes are provided. The italicized title beneath each state name is the official title of that state's body of law.

## ALABAMA
### (Code of Alabama)

**Section 36-26-15.** Tests for establishment of employment registers for positions in classified service; Preferences for veterans, etc.; cooperation of board with federal government, etc.; In establishing and administering standards of personnel qualifications, pay plans, etc.

(a) All persons who have been honorably discharged from the army, navy, air force, marine corps or coast guard who have ever served in the armed forces of the United States at any time shall have five points added to any earned ratings in examinations for entrance to the classified service. All persons who have ever served in the armed forces of the United States at any time who have been honorably discharged and who established by official records of the United States the present existence of a service-connected disability and because of disability are entitled to pension, compensation or disability allowance under existing laws and widows of such persons who shall have died in line of duty during any such period and widows of such persons who shall have been honorably discharged from the army, navy, air force, marine corps or coast guard and wives of such persons who shall have been honorably discharged from the army, navy, air force, marine corps or coast guard who, because of service-connected disability are not themselves qualified but whose wives are qualified, shall have 10 points added to any earned ratings. In entering upon registers the names of preference claimants entitled to five additional points, they will take the place to which their ratings entitle them on the register with non-veterans (the earned ratings augmented by the five points to which they are entitled) and will be certified when their ratings are reached. The name of a veteran with the augmented rating is entered ahead of the name of a non-veteran when their ratings are the same. The names of persons entitled to a 10 point preference, however, will be placed ahead of all others on the register with the same rating (ahead of veterans entitled to a five-point preference and non-veterans) and shall then be certified in the order of their augmented ratings. An appointing officer who passes over a veteran eligible and selects a non-veteran with the same or lower rating shall file with the director the reasons for so doing, which reasons will become a part of the veteran's record but will not be made available to anyone other than the veteran himself, except in the discretion of the appointing officer. When reductions are being made in any part of the classified service, persons entitled to military preference in appointment shall be the last to be discharged or dropped or reduced in rank or salary if their record is good or if their efficiency rating is equal to that of any employee in competition with them who is retained in the service of their department.

(c) The board shall, in establishing and administering standards of personnel qualifications, pay plans and tests both for personnel now in place as well as that later employed, cooperate with and avail itself fully of the advice and assistance of the appointing authorities involved and of the federal government in those departments administered in whole or in part with federal funds.

# ALASKA
## (Alaska Statutes)

Sec. 39.25.159. Employment preference for veterans and prisoners of war

(a) A veteran or prisoner of war who possesses the necessary qualifications for a job classification applied for under this chapter is entitled to a preference under this subsection. In an examination to determine the qualification of applicants for the classified service under merit system examination, five points shall be added to the passing grade of a veteran, 10 points shall be added to the grade of a disabled veteran, or 10 points shall be added to the passing grade of a prisoner of war. A person may receive preference points under only one of these categories. A person may use the preference without limitation when being considered for a position for which persons who are not currently state employees are being considered. If consideration of applicants is limited to state employees, preference points under this subsection may not be counted. If a position in the classified service is eliminated, employees shall be released in accordance with rules that give due effect to all factors. If all job qualifications are equal, a veteran or prisoner of war shall be given preference over a person who was not a veteran or prisoner of war and the veteran or prisoner of war shall be kept on the job. This subsection may not be interpreted to amend the terms of a collective bargaining agreement.

(b) Repealed.

(c) In this section,

(1) "disabled veteran" means a veteran who is entitled to compensation under laws administered by the United States Department of Veterans Affairs, a person who was honorably discharged or released from active duty because of a service-connected disability, or a person who was disabled in the line of duty while serving in the Alaska Territorial Guard;

(2) "prisoner of war" means a person who has been a prisoner of war during a declared war or other conflict as determined by the Department of Defense under federal regulations;

(3) "veteran" means a person

(A) with 181 days or more active service in the armed forces of the United States who has been honorably discharged after having served during any period

(i) between April 6, 1917, and December 1, 1919, between September 16, 1940, and December 31, 1947, or between June 27, 1950, and October 14, 1976; or

(ii) in which the person was awarded a campaign badge, expedition medal, the Purple Heart, or an award or decoration for heroism or gallantry in action;

(B) who served 181 days or more in the Alaska Territorial Guard.

# ARIZONA
## (Arizona Revised Statutes)

## ARTICLE 7. Civil service preference for veterans

### Section 38-491. Eligibility; age limit

The state, or any political subdivision of the state which employs personnel of any branch of its service under a merit system, civil service system or other system of employment on the basis of merit, by whatever name known, and whether pursuant to law, ordinance, rule, regulation or otherwise, shall provide that a veteran of the armed forces of the United States as defined by Title 37, Chapter 1, sec. 101, United States Code, separated from active duty under honorable conditions, shall be eligible to apply for and receive employment under such merit system regardless of age, if otherwise qualified, subject only to the requirement that he is below the regular retirement age at the time of entering the employment, if a retirement age is prescribed.

### Section 38-492. Points of Preference

A. A veteran of the armed forces of the United States separated from the armed forces under honorable conditions following more than six months of active duty, who takes an examination for employment by the state or any political subdivision under a merit system of employment as provided by sec. 38-491 shall, in the determination of the veteran's final rating on such examination, be given a preference of five points over persons other than veterans. The preference shall be added to the grade earned by such veteran, but only if such veteran earns a passing grade without preference.

B. A handicapped person who takes an examination for employment by the state or any political subdivision under a merit system of employment shall, in the determination of the handicapped person's final rating on such examination, be given a preference of five points. The preference shall be added to the grade earned by the handicapped person but only if such person earns a passing grade without preference.

C. A person qualified for a preference pursuant to subsections A and B of this section shall be given a ten point preference.

D. A spouse or surviving spouse of any of the following, otherwise qualified pursuant to subsection A of this section, shall be given a five point preference as if such spouse or surviving spouse were an eligible veteran pursuant to subsection A of this section:

1. Any veteran who died of a service-connected disability.

2. Any member of the armed forces serving on active duty who, at the time of application is listed by the secretary of defense of the United States in any of the following categories for not less than ninety days:

(a) Missing in action.

(b) Captured in the line of duty by a hostile force.

(c) Forcibly detained or interned in the line of duty by a foreign government or power.

3. A person who has a total, permanent disability resulting from a service-connected disability or any person who died while such disability was in existence.

# ARKANSAS
## (Arkansas Code)

**Section 17-1-101.** Examination credit for United States veterans and nurses

(a) In all examinations held by any and all state boards, commissions, or bureaus for the purpose of examining applicants for any license or permit to engage in any profession, trade, or employment, all applicants for such examinations who are veterans of the Army, Navy, Marines, or Nurses of the United States shall have a credit of ten percent (10%) over and above all applicants who are not such veterans or nurses.

(b) The only requirement on the part of the applicant for examination to secure credit of ten percent (10%) shall be the delivery to the examining board, commission, or bureau of the original or a duly and properly executed certified copy of an honorable discharge from the Army, Navy, Marines, or Nurses of the United States.

(c) The advantage given to veterans or nurses under and by this section shall be the same as is given to such veterans and nurses by the acts of Congress for federal positions and licenses.

# CALIFORNIA
## (California Code)

**Section 18950.** Filling of vacancies by promotion; promotional lists; persons on reemployment lists; transfer of eligibility

Vacancies in positions shall be filled insofar as consistent with the best interests of the state from among employees holding positions in appropriate classes, and appropriate promotional lists shall be established to facilitate this purpose, except as provided in Section 18930. Examination shall be held on an open, non-promotional basis when, in the judgment of the board, open competition will produce eligible lists with more highly skilled qualified candidates and is consistent with the best interests of the state.

**Section 18972.** Specific services or employments; permanently disabled veterans; preferential ratings

For specific services or employments as determined by the board, it may in examination allow general or individual preference in ratings to veterans who have suffered permanent disability in line of duty, if such disability will not prevent the proper performance of the duties required under such service or employment, and if such disability is of record in the files of the United States Veterans Administration.

**Section 18973.** Other entrance examinations; additional credits to veterans, widows or widowers of veterans, and spouses of 100 percent disabled veterans; definitions

In the case of all other entrance examinations, a veteran with 30 days or more of service and widows or widowers of veterans who become eligible for certification from eligible lists by attaining the passing mark established for the examination, shall be allowed one of the following additional credits:

(a) Disabled veterans, 15 points.

(b) All other veterans, widows or widowers of veterans, and spouses of 100 percent disabled veterans, 10 points.

For the purpose of this section, "veteran" means any person who has served full time for 30 days or more in the armed forces in time of war or in time of peace in a campaign or expedition for service in which a medal has been authorized by the government of the United States, or during the period September 16, 1940, to January 31, 1955, or who has served at least 181 consecutive days since January 31, 1955, and who has been discharged or released under conditions other than dishonorable, but does not include any person who served only in auxiliary or reserve components of the armed forces whose service therein did not exempt him or her from the operation of the Selective Training and Service Act of 1940.

For the purpose of this section the termination of World War II shall be considered as of midnight, December 31, 1946.

For the purpose of this section: "disabled veteran" means any veteran as defined herein who is currently declared by the United States Veterans Administration to be 10 percent or more disabled as a result of his or her service; and "100 percent disabled veteran" means any veteran as defined herein who is currently declared by the United States Veterans Administration to be 100 percent disabled as a result of his or her service. Proof of disability shall be deemed conclusive if it is of record in the United States Veterans Administration.

**Section 18974.** Addition of credit to percentage attained in examination; placing of names on list; eligibility for appointment; ties

Such credit shall be added to the percentage attained in the examination by the veteran, widow or widower. The name of each shall be placed on the eligible list and he or she is eligible for appointment in the order and on the basis of the percentage attained in examination after the appropriate credit has been added. All ties shall be decided in favor of veterans and widows or widowers of veterans.

**Section 18974.5.** Passage of examination by member of armed forces; subsequent qualification for veterans' preference

Any member of the armed forces who successfully passes any state civil service examination and whose name as a result is placed on an employment list and who within six months after the establishment of the employment list for which such examination was given qualifies for veteran's preference as provided for in Section 18973 shall be allowed the appropriate veterans' credit to the same effect as though he or she were entitled to said credit at the time of the establishing of such employment list. When and if such person is allowed veterans' credit under this section his or her name shall be placed on such employment list in accordance with section 18973 as the employment list stands at the time of qualifying for veterans' credit.

# COLORADO
## (Colorado Constitution)

### Article 12, Section 15. Veterans' Preference

(1)(a) The passing grade on each competitive examination shall be the same for each candidate for appointment or employment in the personnel system of the state or in any comparable civil service or merit system of any agency or political subdivision of the state, including any municipality chartered or to be chartered under article XX of this constitution.

(b) Five points shall be added to the passing grade of each candidate on each such examination, except any promotional examination, who is separated under honorable conditions and who, other than for training purposes, (i) served in any branch of the armed forces of the United States during any period of any declared war or any undeclared war or other armed hostilities against an armed foreign enemy, or (ii) served on active duty in any such branch in any campaign or expedition for which a campaign badge is authorized.

(c) Ten points shall be added to the passing grade of any candidate of each such examination, except any promotional examination, who has so served, other than for training purposes, and who, because of disability incurred in the line of duty, is receiving monetary compensation or disability retired benefits by reason of public laws administered by the department of defense or the veterans administration, or any successor thereto.

(d) Five points shall be added to the passing grade of any candidate of each such examination, except any promotional examination, who is the unremarried widow of any person who was or would have been entitled to additional points under paragraph (b) or (c) of this subsection, or of any person who died during such service or as a result of service-connected cause while on active duty in such branch, other than for training purposes.

(e) No more than a total of ten points shall be added to the passing grade of any such candidate pursuant to this subsection (1).

(2) The certificate of the department of defense or of the veterans administration, or any successor thereto, shall be conclusive proof of service under honorable conditions or of disability or death incurred in the line of duty during such service.

(3)(a) When a reduction in the work force of the state or any such political subdivision thereof becomes necessary because of lack of work or curtailment of funds, employees not eligible for added points under subsection (1) of this section shall be separated before those so entitled who have the same or more service in the employment of the state or such political subdivision, counting both military service for which such points are added and such employment with the state or such political subdivision, as the case may be, from which the employee is to be separated.

(c) In the case of such a person eligible for added points who has completed twenty or more years of active military service, no military service shall be counted in determining length of service in respect to such retention rights. In the case of such a person who has completed less than twenty years of such military service, no more than ten years of service under subsection (1)(b)(i) and (ii) shall be counted in determining such length of service for such retention rights.

(4) The state personnel board and each comparable supervisory or administrative board of any such civil service or merit system of any agency of the state or any such political subdivision thereof, shall implement the provisions of this section to assure that all persons entitled to added points and preference in examinations and retention shall enjoy their full privileges and rights granted by this section.

(5) Any examination which is a promotional examination, but which is also open to persons other than employees for whom such appointment would be a promotion, shall be considered a promotional examination for the purposes of this section.

(6) Any other provision of this section to the contrary notwithstanding, no person shall be entitled to the addition of points under this section for more than one appointment or employment with the same jurisdiction, personnel system, civil service, or merit system.

(7) This section shall be in full force and effect on and after July 1, 1971, and shall grant veterans' preference to all persons who have served in the armed forces of the United States in any declared or undeclared war, conflict, engagement, expedition, or campaign for which a campaign badge has been authorized, and who meet the requirements of service or disability, or both, as provided in this section. This section shall apply to all public employment examinations, except promotional examinations, conducted on or after such date, and it shall be in all respects self-executing.

# CONNECTICUT
## (Connecticut General Statutes)

**Section 5-224.** Credit for military service on examinations

Any veteran who served in time of war, if such veteran is not eligible for disability compensation or pension from the United States through the

Veterans' Administration, or the spouse of such veteran who by reason of such veteran's disability is unable to pursue gainful employment, or the unremarried surviving spouse of such veteran, and if such person has attained at least the minimum earned rating on any examination held for the purpose of establishing an employment list, as provided in section 5-216, shall have five points added to his or her earned rating. Any such veteran, or the spouse of such veteran who by reason of such veteran's disability is unable to pursue gainful employment, or the unremarried surviving spouse of such veteran, if such person is eligible for such disability compensation or pension and if he or she has attained at least the minimum earned rating on any such examination, shall have ten points added to his or her earned rating. Any person who has been honorably discharged from or released under honorable conditions from active service in the Armed Forces of the United States, and who has served in a military action for which such person received or was entitled to receive a campaign badge or expeditionary medal, shall have five points added to his or her earned rating if such person has attained at least the minimum earned rating on any such examination and such person is not otherwise eligible to receive rating points pursuant to this section. Names of any such persons shall be placed upon the lists of eligibles in the order of such augmented ratings. Credits shall be based upon examinations with a possible rating of one hundred points.


# DELAWARE
## (Delaware Code)

**Section 5935.** Veterans' preference

The rules shall provide for preference to be given to veterans of the armed forces of the United States who served during wartime, and who were Delaware residents at the time of their induction. Such rules shall provide that:

(1) Preference shall be confined to original entrance and shall not be applied to promotion within the classified service or to retention in case of reduction in force;

(2) Preference shall be granted only in the form of credits to be added to earned ratings in examinations, with disabled veterans receiving no more than ten points and other veterans no more than five points;

(3) A definition of a disabled veteran shall be set forth in the rules;

(4) All veterans shall be required to obtain a passing examination mark before receiving preference credits;

(5) Employees in the classified service who, while in good standing, leave or have left the state service to engage in military service shall be given credit for seniority purposes for the time served in the armed forces not to exceed three years; and

(6) Any preference points for which a veteran would qualify after complying with subdivisions (1), (2) and (3) of this subsection may be claimed by his or her unremarried widow or widower providing he or she achieves a passing examination grade.

### Section 5937. Preference for residents

The rules shall provide for preference to be given residents of this state in any case where two or more equally qualified persons are concerned.

# DISTRICT OF COLUMBIA
## (District of Columbia Code)

### Section 1-607.3. Veterans preference in employment

(a) For appointment under the provisions of subchapters VIII and IX of this chapter, persons who have served on active duty in the armed forces of the United States for more than 180 consecutive days, not including service under honorable conditions as provided under sec. 511 (d) of Title 10 of the United States Code and have been separated from the armed forces under honorable conditions may receive an additional 5 points on any register established under the authority of subchapters VIII and IX of this chapter.

(b) A person entitled to preference points, as provided in subsection (a) of this section, shall receive an additional 5 points if she or he has separated from the armed forces under honorable conditions, and has established the presence at the time of appointment of a service-connected disability or is receiving compensation, disability retirement benefits, or pensions because of a public law administered by the Veterans Administration or a military department.

(c) Any employee of the District government who, on January 1, 1979, was entitled to veterans preference under federal law, shall continue to be entitled to such veterans preference under this chapter.

(d) The mayor is authorized to develop procedures for the consideration of granting veterans preference, as provided in this section, to persons who served in the armed forces but were less than honorably discharged. Such persons may be entitled to the preference afforded by this section at the time of initial appointment if they show, to the satisfaction of the Mayor, that they have been discriminated against in violation of those rights guaranteed in sec. 1-602.1(2) and this subchapter. No appeal shall be available to any person not afforded a veterans preference under the provisions of this subsection.

(e) Except for the appointment preferences provided in subsections (h), (i), (j), and (k) of this section, no person shall receive any appointment preference after 5 years from the date of separation from the armed forces of the United States.

(f) No person entering the armed forces of the United States after October 14, 1976 shall receive any preference unless the person served in the armed forces of the United States during time of war.

(g) No person retiring from the armed forces of the United States shall receive any preference.

(h) The unmarried widow or widower of a veteran shall be accorded the same preference in appointment as would be accorded to him or her in the federal service pursuant to 5 U. S. C. 2108 (3)(D) and 3309 (1).

(i) The wife or husband of a service-connected disabled veteran shall be accorded the same preference in appointment as would be accorded to her or him in the federal service pursuant to 5 U. S. C. Sec. 2108 (3)(E) and 3309 (1).

(j) A person classified as 30 percent or more disabled under subsection (b) of this section shall receive an appointment preference as provided in that subsection.

(k) A person who served during the Vietnam conflict, who has a discharge of other than dishonorable, shall receive an appointment preference for a period not to exceed 10 years from May 19, 1982.

## FLORIDA
### (Florida Statutes)

**Section 110.2135.** Exemption from examination and hiring procedures; eligible disabled veterans; Probationary employment

(1) An honorably discharged veteran who has wartime service as specified in sec.1.01(14), who has a service-connected disability rated at 30 percent or more by the Veterans Administration or the Armed Services of the United States, and who is a legal resident of this state may be employed by a state agency in a competitive or non-competitive position and is exempt from entrance examination requirements and hiring procedures administered by the Department of Management Services as long as the veteran meets the minimum eligibility requirements for the particular position, or the veteran has been certified by vocational rehabilitation as an appropriate candidate for the position.

(2) A disabled veteran employed under the provisions of subsection (1) shall be appointed for a probationary period of one year. At the end of such period, if the work of the veteran has been satisfactorily performed, the veteran will acquire permanent employment status and will be subject to the employment rules of the Department of Management Services and the veteran's employing agency.

### Section 1.01(14). Veteran defined

(14) The term "veteran" means a person who served in the active military, naval or air service and who was discharged or released therefrom under honorable conditions only or who later received an upgraded discharge under honorable conditions, notwithstanding any action by the Veterans Administration on individuals discharged or released with other than honorable discharges. To receive benefits as a wartime veteran, a veteran must have served during one of the following periods of wartime service:

(a) Spanish-American War: April 21, 1898, to July 4, 1902, and including the Philippine Insurrection and the Boxer Rebellion;

(b) Mexican Border Period: May 9, 1916, to April 5, 1917, in the case of a veteran who during such period served in Mexico, on the borders thereof, or in the waters adjacent thereto;

(c) World War I: April 6, 1917, to November 11, 1918, extended to April 1, 1920 for those veterans who served in Russia; also extended to July 1, 1921 for those veterans who served after November 11, 1918 and before July 2, 1921, provided such veterans had at least one day of service between April 5, 1917 and November 12, 1918;

(d) World War II: December 7, 1941 to December 31, 1946;

(e) Korean Conflict: June 27, 1950 to January 31, 1955;

(f) Vietnam Conflict: August 5, 1964 to May 7, 1975.

# GEORGIA
## (Official Code of Georgia)

**Section 45-2-21.** Veteran entitled to additional five points on civil service examination score

Any veteran who has served on active duty as a member of the armed forces of the United States for a period of more than 180 days, not counting service under an initial period of active duty for training under the six months reserve or national guard programs, any portion of which service occurred during a period of armed conflict in which any branch of the armed forces of the United States engaged, whether under United States command or otherwise, and who was honorably discharged therefrom shall be entitled to and shall have five points added to his passing score on any competitive civil service examination for employment with the state government or any political subdivision thereof; provided however that such veteran is not already eligible for veterans preference under Article IV, Section III, Paragraph II of the Constitution of Georgia.

**Section 45-2-22.** Disabled veteran entitled to additional ten points on civil service examination score.

Any veteran as provided in Code Section 45-2-21 who has at least a ten percent service-connected disability, as rated and certified by the United States Department of Veterans Affairs, shall be entitled to and shall have ten points added to his passing score on any competitive civil service examination, said ten-point preference being in lieu of and not in addition to any other similar preference accorded by law.

# HAWAII
## (Hawaii Revised Statutes)

**Section 76-103.** Veteran's preference

The extent to which veteran's preference shall be given to veterans, to disabled veterans, to spouses of disabled veterans, and to surviving spouses of deceased servicemen who have not remarried shall be provided by rules and regulations.

**Section 363-1.** Definitions

Unless the context clearly requires a different meaning, when used in this chapter:

"Dependent" of a veteran means any person who received from a veteran the person's principal support prior to entry or following entry of the veteran into any of the armed services or following the veteran's discharge from any of the armed services. It includes a dependent of a person currently serving in the service and a former dependent of a discharged or deceased veteran and of a person who has died in such service. It shall not include a dependent of a person discharged under other than honorable conditions.

"Family" of a veteran means members of the immediate family of the veteran, or of a person currently serving in any of the armed services, or of a person who has died in the service, or of a deceased veteran.

"Veteran" means any person who has served in any of the armed services of the United States, or any person who is now a citizen of these United States who has served in any of the armed services of any country which was an ally of the United States in any war or campaign in which the United States was also engaged.

*(Hawaii Personnel Regulations)*

"Applicants must qualify with at least a minimum rating for each part of a civil service examination. An additional credit of five or ten points preference shall be awarded as follows:

(1) Five points preference shall be awarded to honorably separated veterans who served in the armed forces of the United States during any of the following periods:

(A) During the period December 7, 1941 to July 1, 1955;

(B) For more than 180 consecutive days from January 31, 1955 through October 14, 1976 (not including active duty for training under Reserve or National Guard program); or

(C) In a campaign or expedition for which a campaign badge or service medal has been authorized;

(2) Ten points preference shall be awarded to:

(A) Honorably separated veterans with a service-connected disability, included those awarded the Purple Heart;

(B) The spouse of an honorably separated veteran with a service-connected disability which disqualifies the veteran for State positions in his/her usual occupation; or

(C) An unremarried, surviving spouse of a person who died while on

43

active duty, or of an honorably separated veteran who served during the periods cited above."

# IDAHO
## (Code of Idaho)

**Section 65-502.** Preference to be given veterans by public employers

In all employment of any kind or character, excluding confidential secretarial positions, in all state, county, and municipal governments and departments and in all political subdivisions thereof, the official person in charge of such unit of government shall give preference to the employment of veterans who served on military duty in the armed forces of the United States for a period of more than one hundred and eighty days or whose discharge or release from military duty was for a disability incurred or aggravated in the line of duty, who are discharged under honorable conditions, and who are residents of the State of Idaho when the application for work or employment is made.

An application for an examination for appointment to a position in said public employment will be accepted after the closing date of the examination from a person who was serving in the armed forces, or undergoing hospitalization of no more than one year following discharge during any period in which the examination was open. The application must be submitted within one hundred twenty days of her or his separation from the armed forces or hospitalization and prior to the expiration of any register established as a result of the examination. A disabled veteran may file an application at any time for any position for which a register is then maintained, or for which a register is about to be established, provided she or he has not already been examined twice for the same position and grade for which application is made, does not have current eligibility on that register, or is not serving in a competitive position in the same grade for which application is made.

**Section 65-506.** Addition of points to competitive examination ratings

Five points shall be added to the earned rating of any war veteran and the widow of any war veteran as long as she remains unmarried, when required to take competitive examination for any position in any state department, county or municipal government, which may now or which

44

may hereafter require competitive examination under merit system or civil service plan of selecting employees. The names of all five point preference eligibles resulting from any merit system or civil service examination shall be placed on the register in accordance with their augmented rating.

Ten points shall be added to the earned rating of any disabled war veteran, the widow of any disabled war veteran as long as she remains unmarried, the wife of any disabled veteran who himself is physically unable to perform the work in the position to which the wife seeks to apply the preference, when required to take competitive examination for any position in any state department, county or municipal government, which may now or which may hereafter require competitive examinations under merit system or civil service plan of selecting employees. The names of all ten point preference eligibles resulting from any merit system or civil service examination shall be placed at the top of the register above the names of all non-preference eligibles in accordance with their augmented ratings.

The additional points added by reason of veteran's preference shall be used only for the purpose of initial appointment and not for the purpose of promotions.

### Section 65-507. Disabled veteran defined

The term "disabled war veteran" as used in this act means an individual who has served on military duty in the armed forces of the United States during any period of war recognized by the United States Department of Veterans Affairs for the purpose of awarding federal benefits as may be defined in Title 38, U. S. C., Chapter 1, sec. 101 (11), and has been separated therefrom under honorable conditions, and has established the present existence of a service-connected disability, and is receiving compensation, disability retirement benefits or pension under public law as administered by the Department of Veterans Affairs or a military department.

# ILLINOIS
## (Illinois Compiled Statutes)

### Section 415.8(b)(7). Veteran's preference credit for service in armed forces

For the granting of appropriate preference in entrance examinations to qualified persons who have been members of the armed forces of the United States, were members of the armed forces of allies of the United States in time of hostilities with a foreign country, and to certain other persons as set forth in this section.

(a) As used in this section:

(1) "Time of hostilities with a foreign country" means any period of time in the past, present or future during which a declaration of war by the United States Congress has been or is in effect that is recognized by the issuance of a presidential proclamation or a presidential executive order and in which the armed forces expeditionary medal or other campaign service medals are awarded according to presidential executive order.

(2) "Armed forces of the United States" means the U.S. Army, Navy, Air Force, Marine Corps or Coast Guard. Service in the Merchant Marine that constitutes active duty under section 401 of federal Public Law 95-202 shall also be considered service in the armed forces of the United States for the purposes of this section.

(b) The preference granted under this section shall be in the form of points added to the final grades of the persons if they otherwise qualify and are entitled to appear on the list of those eligible for appointments.

(c) A veteran is qualified for a preference of ten points if the veteran currently holds proof of a service-connected disability from the U.S. Department of Veterans Affairs or an allied country or if the veteran is a recipient of the Purple Heart.

(d) A veteran who has served during a time of hostilities with a foreign country is qualified for a preference of five points if the veteran served under one or more of the following conditions:

(1) the veteran served a total of at least six months, or

(2) the veteran served for the duration of hostilities regardless of the length of engagement, or

(3) the veteran was discharged on the basis of hardship, or

(4) the veteran was released from active duty because of a service-connected disability and was discharged under honorable conditions.

(e) A person not eligible for a preference under subsection (c) or (d) is qualified for a preference of three points if the person has served in the armed forces of the United States, the Illinois National Guard, or any reserve component of the armed forces of the United States if the person: (1) served for at least six months and has been discharged under honorable conditions or (2) has been discharged on the ground of hardship, or (3) was released from active duty because of a service-connected disability. An active member of the National Guard or a reserve component of the armed forces of the United States is eligible for the preference if the member meets the service requirements of this subsection.

(f) The rank order of persons entitled to a preference on eligible lists shall be determined on the basis of augmented ratings. When the director establishes eligible lists on the basis of category ratings such as "superior," "excellent," "well-qualified" and "qualified," then the veteran eligibles in each such category shall be preferred for appointment before the non-veteran eligibles in the same category.

(g) Employees in positions covered by jurisdiction B who, while in good standing, leave to engage in military service during a period of hostility, shall be given credit for seniority purposes for time served in the armed forces.

(h) A surviving unremarried spouse of a veteran who suffered a service-connected death or the spouse of a veteran who suffered a service-connected disability which prevents the veteran from qualifying for civil service employment shall be entitled to the same preference to which the veteran would have been entitled under this section.

(i) A preference shall also be given to the following individuals: ten points for one parent of an unmarried veteran who suffered a service-connected death or a service-connected disability that prevents the veteran from qualifying for civil service employment. The first parent to receive a civil service appointment shall be the parent entitled to the preference.

*Section 55.1.* Veterans preference for public works

In the employment and appointment to fill positions in the construction, addition to, or alteration of all public works undertaken or contracted for by the state, or by any political subdivision thereof, preference shall be given to persons who have been members of the armed forces of the United States or who, while citizens of these United States, were members of the armed forces of allies of the United States in time of hostilities with a foreign country, and have served under one or more of the following conditions:

(1) the veteran served a total of at least six months, or

(2) the veteran served for the duration of hostilities regardless of the length of the engagement, or

(3) the veteran served in a theater of operations but was discharged on the basis of hardship, or

(4) the veteran was released from active duty because of a service-connected disability and was honorably discharged. But such preference shall only be given to those persons who are found to possess the business capacity necessary for the proper discharge of the duties of such employment. No political subdivision or person contracting for such public works is required to give preference to veterans who are not residents of such district over residents thereof who are not veterans

# INDIANA
## (Indiana Statutes)

**Section 4-15-2-18.** Rating of completed test; Method; Preference to veterans or their widows; Procedure to obtain preference

(b) In certification for appointment, in appointment, in reinstatement, and in reemployment in any state service, preference shall be given to former members of the military services of the United States who served on active duty in any branch of the armed forces and who at no time received a discharge or separation under other than honorable conditions, except corrected separation or discharge to read "honorable" as evidenced by appropriate records presented from the U.S. Department of Defense or appropriate branch of the military service.

(c) Preference shall be given in the following priorities:

(1) Former members of the military service who have established the present existence of a service-connected disability of ten percent or more, as evidenced by records of the U.S. Department of Veterans Affairs or disability retirement benefits as evidenced by laws administered by the U.S. Department of Defense.

(2) The spouse of such service-connected disabled veterans and the unremarried spouse of deceased Veterans;

(3) Those former members of the military service who are wartime veterans;

(4) Veterans of the military service who served more than one hundred eighty-one days on active duty regardless of when served;

(d) In all written examinations to determine the qualifications of applicants for entrance into the state service:

(1) ten points shall be added to the earned rating of persons taking competitive examination under subsection (c)(1) or (c)(2);

(2) five points shall be added to the earned rating of persons taking competitive examination under subsection (c)(3); and

(3) two points shall be added to the earned rating of persons taking competitive examination under subsection (c)(4).

(e) All points specified in subsection (d) shall be added to the total combined test scores of the person and shall not be allocated to any single feature or part of the competitive examination. Rating shall be based on a scale of one hundred points as the maximum attainable.

(f) When veterans preference in state service employment is limited to wartime veterans, this subsection applies for the purpose of defining "war":

(1) World War II—December 7, 1941 to December 31, 1946;

(2) Korean Conflict—June 27, 1950 to January 31, 1955;

(3) Vietnam Conflict—August 5, 1964 to May 7, 1975;

(4) Actual combat or duty equally hazardous, regardless of time, or service in any foreign war, insurrection or expedition, which service is recognized by the award of a service or campaign medal of the United States;

(5) Participation as a regularly assigned crew member of any military craft in a mission in support of a military operation, regardless of time, as designated by the armed forces of the United States.

(g) Active duty consists of:

(1) ninety days or more of wartime service;

(2) ninety days or more of consecutive service which began or ended during wartime period

(3) ninety days or more of combined service in two or more wartime periods;

(4) service of less than ninety days, if discharged for a disability in the line of duty; or

(5) service qualifying under subsection (f)(4) or (f)(5) which must be documented by appropriate records of the U.S. Department of Defense.

(h) In examinations where experience is an element of qualification, time spent in the armed forces of the United States shall be credited in a veteran's rating where the veteran's actual employment in a vocation similar to that for which the veteran is examined was interrupted by such service. In all examinations to determine the qualifications of a veteran applicant, credit shall be given for all valuable experience, including experience gained in religious, civic, welfare, service and organizational activities, regardless of whether any compensation was received for the experience.

(i) In determining qualifications for examination, appointment, promotion, retention, transfer, or reinstatement, with respect to preference eligibles the department shall waive requirements as to height, age and weight if the requirement is not essential to the performance of the duties of the position for which examination is given. The department, after giving due consideration to the recommendation of any accredited physician, shall waive the physical requirements in the case of any veteran if the veteran is, in the opinion of the director, physically able to discharge efficiently the duties of the position for which examination is given. No minimum educational requirement may be prescribed in any civil service examination except for such scientific, technical or professional positions, the duties of which the department decides cannot be performed by a person who does not have such education. The director shall make a part of the department's public records the director's reasons for such decision.

(j) The names of preference eligibles shall be entered on the appropriate registers or lists of eligibles in accordance with their respective augmented ratings. The name of a preference eligible shall be entered ahead of all others having the same rating.

(k) The director shall adopt appropriate rules under Section 4-22-2 for the administration and enforcement of this section.

(l) In any reduction in personnel in any state service, competing employees shall be released in accordance with board regulations which shall give due effect to tenure of employment, military preference, length of service and efficiency ratings. The length of time spent in the active service in the armed forces of the United States of each such employee shall be credited in computing the total length of service. Veteran's preference points shall be added to the retention score of a preference eligible. When any of the functions of any state agency are transferred to, or when any state agency is replaced by some other state agency or agencies, all preference employees in the function or functions so transferred or in the agency replaced shall first be transferred to the replacing agency or agencies for employment in positions for which they are qualified, before the agency or agencies appoint additional employees from any other sources for such positions.

(m) Any preference eligible who has resigned may, at the request of any appointing officer, be certified for and appointed to any position for which the preference eligible has been a regular employee in the state service.

(n) Any preference eligible who has been furloughed or separated without delinquency or misconduct, upon request, shall have the preference eligible's name placed on all appropriate registers and employment lists for every position for which the preference eligible's qualifications have been established.

(o) Applicants who claim preference of their own service must submit either:

(1) original discharge or separation, or certified copies or photostat copies of the originals;

(2) an official statement from the U.S. Department of Defense showing record of service; or

(3) an official statement from the Department of Veterans Affairs supporting a claim for disability.

# IOWA
## (Iowa Code)

**Section 35 C.1.** Appointments and employment—applications

1. In every public department and upon all public works in the state, and of counties, cities and school corporations of the state, honorably discharged persons from the military or naval forces of the United States in any war in which the United States has been engaged, including the Korean Conflict at any time between June 25, 1950 and January 31, 1955, both dates inclusive, and the Vietnam Conflict beginning on August 5, 1964 and ending on May 7, 1975, both dates inclusive, and the Persian Gulf War beginning on August 2, 1990 and ending on the date specified by the president or the Congress of the United States as the date of permanent cessation of hostilities, both dates inclusive, who are citizens and residents of this state are entitled to preference in appointment and employment over other applicants of no greater qualifications. However, if the United States Congress enacts a date different from August 2, 1990 as the beginning of the Persian Gulf War to determine the eligibility of a veteran for military benefits as a veteran of the Persian Gulf War, then the date enacted by the Congress shall be substituted. The preference in appointment and employment for employees of cities under a municipal civil service is the same as that provided in section 400.10. For the purposes of this

section service in World War II means service in the armed forces of the United States between December 7, 1941 and December 31, 1946, both dates inclusive.

2. In all jobs of the state and its political subdivisions, an application form shall be completed. The form shall contain an inquiry into the applicant's military service during the wars or armed conflicts as specified in subsection 1.

3. In all jobs in political subdivisions of the state which are to be filled by competitive examination or by appointment, public notice of the application deadline to fill the job shall be posted at least ten days before the deadline in the same manner as notices of meetings are posted under section 21.4.

4. For jobs in political subdivisions of this state that are filled through a point-rated qualifying examination, the preference afforded to veterans shall be equivalent to that provided for municipal civil service systems in section 400.10.

### Section 400.10. Preferences

In all examinations and appointments under this chapter, other than promotions and appointments of chief of the police department and chief of the fire department, honorably discharged veterans from the military and naval forces of the United States in any war in which the United States has been engaged, including the Korean Conflict at any time between June 25, 1950 and January 31, 1955, both dates inclusive, and the Vietnam War beginning August 5, 1964 and ending May 7, 1975, both dates inclusive, and who are citizens and residents of this state, shall have five points added to the veteran's grade or score attained in qualifying examinations for appointment to positions and five additional points added to the grade or score if the veteran has a service-connected disability or is receiving compensation, disability benefits or pension under laws administered by the Veterans Administration. An honorably discharged veteran who has been awarded the Purple Heart for disabilities incurred in action shall be considered to have a service-connected disability. However, the points shall be given only upon passing the exam and shall not be the determining factor in passing.

# KANSAS
## (Kansas Statutes)

### Section 73-201. Preference in appointments and employments

In grateful recognition of the services, sacrifices and sufferings of persons who served in the army, navy, air force or marine corps of the United States in World War I and World War II, and of persons who have served with the armed forces of the United States during the military, naval and air operations in Korea, Vietnam or other places under the flags of the U.S. and the U.N. or under the flag of the U.S. alone, and have been honorably discharged therefrom, they shall be preferred for appointments and employed to fill positions in every public department and upon all public works of this state, and of the counties and cities of this state, if competent to perform such services; and the persons thus preferred shall not be disqualified from holding any position in said service on account of his age or by reason of any physical or mental disability which does not render him incompetent to perform the duties of the position applied for; and when any such ex-soldier, sailor, airman or marine shall apply for appointment or employment. The officer, board or person whose duty it is or may be to appoint a person to fill such place shall, if the applicant be a man or woman of good reputation, and can perform the duties of the position applied for by him or her, appoint said ex-soldier, sailor, airman or marine to such position, place or employment; **provided,** that the provisions of this act shall not be applicable to any persons classified as conscientious objectors. The provisions of this act shall not be controlling over the provisions of any statute, county resolution or city ordinance relating to retirement or termination on the basis of age, of employees of the state or any county or city. Whenever under any statute, county resolution or city ordinance retirement, or termination on the basis of age, of any employee is required at a certain age, or is optional with the employer at a certain age, such provisions of such statute, resolution or ordinance, shall be controlling and shall not be limited by this section.

### Section 75-2955. Veterans' preference

In all examinations under this act, veterans' preference shall be given to all persons separated from the armed services under honorable conditions who served on active duty during any war. The official dates for war service are April 6, 1917 through July 2, 1921; December 7, 1941 through April 28, 1952; the period April 28, 1952 through July 1, 1955; in any campaign or expedition for which a campaign badge or service medal has been authorized; or for more than 180 consecutive days since January 31, 1955. An initial period of active duty for training under the "six month" reserve or national guard program shall not count toward the one hundred and eighty consecutive day requirement. Persons entering the armed services on or after October 15, 1976 shall not be entitled to veterans' preference based on that period of service unless awarded a service medal or a campaign badge. A veteran shall include any person who has voluntarily retired with twenty or more years of active service. Veterans' preference points and dates shall be applicable only to examinations given on or after the effective date of this act and shall not be applied retroactively.

To the final earned rating of all such veterans as defined herein who shall have attained a passing rating on any open competitive examination, there shall be added a credit of five points, and in the case of a disabled veteran there shall be added a total credit of ten points. No disabled veteran shall be entitled to the additional benefits herein provided unless such service was during an accepted period, as defined herein, and such disability is at the time of examination rated by the United States Veterans Administration as being service-connected and not less than ten percent.

# KENTUCKY
## (Kentucky Revised Statutes)

**Section 18A.150.** Preference points for honorably discharged members of the armed forces, their spouses, surviving spouses and parents; present and former members of the Kentucky National Guard

(1) Any honorably discharged soldier, sailor, marine, member of the Air Force or member of any other branch of the military service who was inducted into that service through voluntary or involuntary enlistment, shall have five points added to his entrance examination score for classified positions. Any Kentucky National Guard member, or a former member of the Kentucky National Guard who has been honorably discharged shall be entitled to the same number of points.

(2) Any honorably discharged soldier, sailor, marine, member of the Air Force or member of any other branch of the military service who was inducted into that service through voluntary or involuntary enlistment, who the United States Veterans Administration or any branch of the armed forces of the United States determines has service-connected disabilities, shall have ten points added to his entrance examination score for a classified position.

(3) The spouse of an honorably discharged soldier, sailor, marine, member of the Air Force or member of any other branch of the military service who was inducted into that service through voluntary or involuntary enlistment who would be eligible for a ten-point preference, and whose

service-connected disability disqualifies him for positions along the general line of his usual occupation shall have ten preference points added to his entrance examination score for a classified position In such a case, the spouse loses the right to preference if the disabled veteran recovers.

(4) Until remarriage, the surviving spouse of an honorably discharged soldier, sailor, marine, member of the Air Force or member of any other branch of the military service who was inducted into that service through voluntary or involuntary enlistment, shall have ten preference points added to his entrance examination score for a classified position. This includes the surviving spouse of any military personnel who died while in the armed forces, unless circumstances surrounding the death would have been cause for other than honorable discharge or separation.

(5) A parent totally or partially dependent on a soldier, sailor, marine, member of the Air Force or member of any other branch of the military service who was inducted into that service through voluntary or involuntary enlistment, and who lost his life under honorable conditions while on active duty or active duty for training purposes, or who became permanently and totally disabled as a result of a service-connected disability, shall have ten preference points added to his examination score for a classified position.

(6) The preference points granted by subsections (1) through (5) of this section shall be added to entrance examination scores for classified positions only if the score is determined by the commissioner to be a passing score and after the verification of the required service. The total of the entrance examination score and the preference points shall not exceed one hundred.

# LOUISIANA
## (Louisiana Revised Statutes)
## (Louisiana Constitution)

### Constitution Article 10, Section 10 (2). Veterans

The state and city civil service departments shall accord a five-point preference in original appointment to each person who served honorably in the armed forces of the United States during a war declared by the United States Congress, or in a peacetime campaign or expedition for which campaign badges are authorized, or during war period dates or dates of armed conflicts as provided by state law enacted by two-thirds of the elected members of each house of the legislature. The state and city civil service departments shall accord a ten-point preference in original appointment to each honorably discharged veteran who served either in peace or in war and who has one or more disabilities recognized as service-connected by the Veterans Administration; to the spouse of each veteran whose physical condition precludes his or her appointment to a civil service job in his or her usual line of work; to the unremarried widow of each deceased veteran who served in a war period, as defined above, or in a peacetime campaign or expedition; or to the unremarried widowed parent of any person who died in active wartime or peacetime service or who suffered total and permanent disability in active wartime or peacetime service; or to the divorced or separated parents of any person who died in wartime or peacetime service or who became permanently and totally disabled in wartime or peacetime service. However, only one ten-point preference shall be allowed in the original appointment to any person enumerated above. If the ten-point preference is not used by the veteran, either because of the veteran's physical or mental incapacity which precludes his appointment to a civil service job in his usual line of work or because of his death, then the preference shall be available to his spouse, unremarried widow, or eligible parents as defined above, in the order specified. However, any such preference may be given only to a person who has attained at least the minimum score required on each test and who has received at least the minimum rating required for eligibility.

### Section (3). Layoffs; preference employees

When a position in the classified service is abolished or needs to be vacated because of stoppage of work from lack of funds or other causes, then preference employees (ex-members of the armed forces and their dependents as described in this section) whose length of service and efficiency ratings are at least equal to those of other competing employees shall be retained in preference to other employees. However, when any function of a state agency is transferred to, or when a state agency is replaced by, one or more other state agencies, then every preference employee in classifications and performing functions transferred, or working in the state agency replaced, shall be transferred to the replacing state agency or agencies for employment in a position for which he is qualified before that state agency or agencies appoint additional employees for such positions from eligible lists.

# MAINE
## (Maine Revised Statutes)

**Section 7054.** Veterans' preference

In making appointments to and retention in any position on an open competitive basis in the classified service, preference shall be given to veterans of the Armed Forces of The United States who have been honorably separated, or to their wives, husbands, widows, widowers, mothers or fathers as set forth in this section.

1. Definitions. As used in this section, unless the context otherwise indicates, the following terms have the following meanings:

A. "Armed forces" means the United States Army, Navy, Air Force, Marine Corps or Coast Guard.

B. "Honorable separation" means discharge or release from a continuous tour of active duty in any of the armed forces, the official records of which show the character of service or type of discharge to have been honorable.

C. "Veteran" means a person, male or female, who served on full-time active duty, exclusive for active duty for training, in the armed forces of the United States and who does not have a nondisability retirement pension for armed forces service.

D. "War, campaign or expedition" means any of the following periods:

(1) April 6, 1917 to November 10, 1918;

(2) December 7, 1941 to September 1, 1945;

(3) June 27, 1950 to January 31, 1955; and

(4) August 5, 1964 to May 7, 1975.

2. Examination preference. Preference points shall be added to the earned qualifying rating in examinations, provided that a passing grade is attained, of veterans applying for positions in the state service in accordance with the following, provided that they have not been previously employed in the classified service after obtaining preference points. A veteran who is receiving a disability pension shall be entitled to preference points under this subsection, notwithstanding his previous employment in the classified service after obtaining preference points.

A. A veteran who served on active duty in any of the armed forces for at least ninety consecutive days during a war, campaign or expedition

57

and who was honorably separated shall be accorded a five-point preference. A five-point preference shall also be accorded a veteran who served on active duty in any of the armed forces for at least ninety consecutive days and who, during that time:

(1) served in the expedition to Grenada at any time from October 25, 1983 to November 2, 1983; or

(2) served in the mission to Lebanon at any time from August 25, 1983 to February 24, 1984.

B. The widow or widower of a veteran, as defined in paragraph A, who has never remarried, shall be granted a five-point preference.

C. A veteran who served on active duty in any of the armed forces for at least ninety consecutive days, at any time, was honorably separated, and who has a service-connected disability of ten percent or more and receives compensation, pension or disability retirement under public laws administered by the Veterans Administration or a branch of the armed forces shall be accorded a ten-point preference.

D. The spouse of a disabled veteran as defined in paragraph C, is entitled to a ten-point preference in lieu of the veteran when his or her service-connected disability disqualifies him or her for appointment in the classified service along the general lines of his or her usual occupation.

E. The widow or widower, who has never remarried, of a veteran who lost his or her life under honorable conditions while serving on active duty in any of the armed forces during the war, campaign or expedition, or who died as the result of service-connected disability shall be accorded a ten-point preference.

F. The natural mother or father of a deceased veteran who lost his or her life under honorable conditions while serving on active duty in any of the armed forces during a war, campaign or expedition, and who is or was married to the father or mother of the veteran on whose service he or she bases his or her claim, and who is widowed, divorced or separated, or who lives with him or her totally and permanently disabled husband or wife, either the veteran's father or mother or the husband or wife of his or her remarriage, is entitled to a ten-point preference.

2. Certification preference. Names of preference veterans shall be entered on appropriate registers as follows:

A. The names of five-point preference veterans shall be entered on appropriate registers in accordance with their respective augmented ratings, but they shall be entered ahead of all nonveterans having the same rating.

B. The names of qualified ten-point preference veterans who have a compensable service-connected disability of ten percent or more shall be placed at the top of the appropriate register in accordance with their respective augmented ratings, in nonprofessional and nonscientific classes below range twelve of the compensation plan.

3. Retention preference. In any reduction in personnel in the state service, veteran preference employees shall be retained in preference to all other competing employees in the same classification with equal seniority, status and service ratings.

In determining qualifications for examination and appointment with respect to veteran preference eligibles under this section, the director or other examining agency may waive requirements as to age, height and weight, provided that any such requirement is not essential to the performance of the duties of the position for which examination is given. The director or other examining agency, after giving due consideration to the recommendation of any accredited physician, may waive the physical requirements in the case of any veteran, provided that the veteran is, in the opinion of the director or other examining agency, physically able to discharge efficiently the duties of the position for which examination is given.

This section applies to all examinations for original positions in the state police, Department of Inland Fisheries and Wildlife, Department of Marine Resources, University of Maine system, vocational-technical institutes, Maine School Building Authority, Maine Turnpike Authority, Finance Authority of Maine or any other state or quasi-state agency.

# MARYLAND
## (Code of Maryland)

**Section 7-207.** Credits in selection tests

(a) In general—A credit under this section shall be applied to an applicant's score on any selection test administered to establish placement on a list of eligible candidates for which the applicant is otherwise qualified and has at least the minimum passing score on the selection test.

(b) Current state employees—For a current state employee, an appointing authority shall apply a credit on a selection test, of one-quarter point for each year of service in the state government, up to a maximum of five points for twenty years of state service.

(c) Veterans and spouses of veterans—(1) In this subsection, "eligible veteran" means a veteran of any branch of the armed forces of the United States who has received an honorable discharge or a certificate of satisfactory completion of military service. (2) An appointing authority shall apply a credit of ten points on any selection test for:

    a. an eligible veteran

    b. the spouse of an eligible veteran who has a service-connected disability; or

    c. the surviving spouse of a deceased eligible veteran

(3) The following applicants are ineligible for a credit under this subsection:

    a. a current state employee; and

    b. an eligible veteran who is convicted of a crime after being discharged from or completing military service.

(g) State residents—In the selection process for an appointment to a position within the state Personnel Management System, an appointing authority shall allow five points to each resident of the State.

**Section 48.** Special credits to veterans taking examination for positions in political subdivisions.

In every city, county or other political subdivision of this state in which appointments are made under any civil service or merit system law or ordinance, the commission or board which provides eligible lists for appointment shall promulgate rules or regulations granting special credit or credits to honorably discharged veterans of the military and naval services of the U.S. and who have been residents of this state for five years or more immediately preceding the date on which such veterans take any merit system examination. The said commission or board shall have the power to determine the nature and extent of the special credit or credits to be allowed such veterans and may allow a greater credit or credits to disabled veterans than to non-disabled veterans. The same credit, credits or preference may be extended to the spouses of such veterans as have themselves been unable to qualify for merit system appointment because of disability and to the unmarried surviving spouses of deceased veterans. The rules and regulations of any civil service commission or board may also provide for exempting such war veterans under fifty-five years of age from any age limitation or requirement.

# MASSACHUSETTS
## (Massachusetts General Laws)

**Chapter 31**

**Section 26.** Order of persons on eligible lists; veteran's preference; disabled veterans; fire and police service

The names of persons who pass examination for original appointment to any position in the official service shall be placed on eligible lists in the following order: (1) disabled veterans, in the order of their respective standings; (2) veterans, in the order of their respective standings; (3) widows or widowed mothers of veterans who were killed in action or died from a service-connected disability incurred in wartime service, in the order of their respective standings; (4) all others, in the order of their respective standings. Upon receipt of a requisition, names shall be certified from such lists according to the method of certification prescribed by the rules.

The spouse or single parent of a veteran who was killed in action or died from s service-connected disability incurred in wartime service, upon presenting proof from official sources of such facts, satisfactory to the administrator, and proof that such spouse or parent has not remarried, shall be entitled to the preference provided for in this section.

The administrator may require any disabled veteran to present a certificate of a physician, approved by the administrator, that his disability is not such as to incapacitate him from the performance of the duties of the position for which he is eligible. The cost of a physical examination of such veteran for the purpose of obtaining such certificate shall be borne by the commonwealth.

A person who has received a Congressional Medal of Honor may apply to the administrator for appointment to or employment in a civil service position without examination. In such application he shall state under penalties of perjury the facts required by the rules. Age, loss of limb or other disability which does not in fact incapacitate shall not disqualify him from appointment or employment under this section. Appointing officers may make requisition for the names of any or all such persons and appoint or employ any of them. A person who has received a Distinguished Service Cross or Navy Cross may, upon the recommendation of the administrator and with the approval of the commission, be appointed under the same conditions provided in this paragraph for a person who has received the Medal of Honor.

An appointing authority shall appoint a veteran in making a provisional appointment under section twelve, unless such appointing authority shall have attained from the administrator a list of all veterans who, within the twelve months next preceding, have filed applications for the kind of work called for by such provisional appointment, shall have mailed a notice of the position vacancy to each such veterans and shall have determined that none of such veterans is qualified for or is willing to accept the appointment.

A disabled veteran shall be retained in employment in preference to all other persons, including veterans.

## Chapter 149

*Section 26.* Public works; preference to veterans and citizens; wages

In the employment of mechanics and apprentices, teamsters, chauffeurs and laborers in the construction of public works by the commonwealth, or by a county, town or district, or by persons contracting for subcontracting for such works, preference shall first be given to citizens of the commonwealth who have been residents herein for at least six months at the commencement of their employment who are male veterans as defined in Chapter 4, section 7, clause 43, and who are qualified to perform the work to which the employment relates; and secondly to citizens of this commonwealth generally who have been residents of herein for at least six months at the commencement of their employment, and if they cannot be obtained in sufficient numbers, then to citizens of the United States, and every contract for such work shall contain a provision to this effect. Each county, town or district in the construction of public works, or persons contracting or subcontracting for such works, shall give preference to veterans and citizens who are residents of such county, town or district. The rate per hour of the wages paid to said mechanics and apprentices, teamsters, chauffeurs and laborers in the construction of public works shall not be less than the rate or rates of wages to be determined by the commissioner as hereinafter provided; provided, that the wages paid to laborers employed on said works shall not be less than those paid to laborers in the municipal service of the town or towns where said works are being constructed: provided, further, that where the same public work is to be constructed in two or more towns, the wages paid to laborers shall not be less than those paid to laborers in the municipal service of the town paying the highest rate; provided, further, that if in any of the towns where the works are to be constructed, a wage rate or wage rates have been established in certain trades and occupations by collective agreements or understandings in the private construction industry between organized labor and employers, the rate or rates to be paid on said works shall not be less than the rates so established; provided, further, that in towns where no such rate or rates have been established, the wages paid to mechanics and apprentices, teamsters, chauffeurs and laborers on public works, shall not be less than the wages paid to the employees in the same trades and occupations by private employers engaged in the construction industry.

# MICHIGAN
## (Michigan Compiled Laws)

**Section 35.401.** Veterans preference for public employment; qualifications; county civil service act

Sec. (1). In every public department and upon the public works of this state and of every county and municipal corporation thereof, honorably discharged veterans as defined by Act No. 190 of the public acts of 1965, as amended, being sections 35.61 and 35.62 of the Michigan Compiled Laws, shall be preferred for appointment and employment. Age, loss of limb or other physical impairment which does not in fact incapacitate, shall not be deemed to disqualify them. When it shall become necessary to fill by appointment a vacancy occurring in an elective office, the appointment shall be deemed to be within this Act. The applicant shall be of good moral character and shall have been a resident of this state for at least two years and of the county in which the office or position is located for at least one year, and possess other requisite qualifications, after credit allowed by the provisions of any civil service laws. In any instance where there is a conflict between the provisions of this Act and Act. No. 370 of the Public Acts of 1941, as amended, being sections 38.401 to 38.428 of the Michigan Compiled Laws, the provisions of Act No. 370 of the Public Acts of 1941, as amended, shall prevail.

**Section 35.61.** Definitions; applicable dates and terms

Sec. (1). In order to provide for the uniformity of service dates for veterans, the following sates and terms shall be applicable to all acts of this state relative to veterans:

(a) "Veteran" means a person who served in the active military forces during a period of war or who received the armed forces expeditionary or other campaign service medal during an emergency condition and who was discharged or released therefrom under honorable conditions. "Veteran" also includes a person who died in active military forces.

(b) "Spanish-American War" means the period beginning on April 21, 1898 and ending on July 4, 1902, includes the Philippine Insurrection and the Boxer Rebellion, and in the case of veteran who served with the United States military forces engaged in hostilities in the Moro Province, means the period beginning on April 21, 1898 and ending on July 15, 1903.

(c) "World War I" means the period beginning on April 6, 1917 and ending on November 11, 1918, and in the case of a veteran who served with the United States military forces in Russia, means the period beginning on April 6, 1917 and ending on April 1, 1920.

(d) "World War II" means the period beginning on December 7, 1941 and ending December 31, 1946, both dates inclusive.

(e) "Korean Conflict" means the period between June 27, 1950 to January 31, 1955.

(f) Civil War and confederate veterans who served between April 12, 1861 and May 26, 1865.

(g) Indian Wars. Since the Indian Wars were fought intermittently over a period of years, the determination as to whether a person shall be considered as having rendered military service during these wars will be carefully considered by the state Veterans' Trust Fund. January 1, 1817 through December 31, 1898 is considered the Indian War Period.

(h) Mexican Wars. Since there were several skirmishes involving the Mexican Border such as the Mexican Border troubles from 1911–1916; the Veracruz Expedition into Mexico from March 15, 1916 to February 5, 1917; the persons rendering military service in any of these skirmishes shall be considered veterans of the Mexican Wars between 1911 and February 5, 1917.

(i) Future dates. The period beginning on the date of any future declaration of war by the Congress or the beginning of an emergency condition recognized by the issuance of a Presidential proclamation or a Presidential executive order and in which the armed forces expeditionary medal or other campaign service medals are awarded according to Presidential executive order and ending on a date prescribed by Presidential proclamation or concurrent resolution of the Congress.

(j) Veterans of the Korean Conflict and veterans having served after January 31, 1955 in an area of hazardous duty for which an armed forces expeditionary or Vietnam Service Medal was received or veterans having served in the Vietnam Era which is defined as that period beginning August 5, 1964 and ending on May 7, 1975.

# MICHIGAN
## (Michigan Personnel Regulations)

**Reg. 2-5.1.** Definition: Veterans; Disabled veterans

A veteran is any person who has had not less than ninety (90) calendar days of active service in the armed forces of the United States during any period covered by a selective service law and who has received an honorable discharge or other suitable evidence of honorable active service. A person, other than a disabled veteran, who has retired from any branch of the armed forces is ineligible for veterans' preference. A disabled veteran is one who the Veterans Administration or any branch of the military has determined to be eligible for receiving disability compensation.

**Reg. 2-5.2.** Preference credit points.—preference credit will be applied as follows:

(a) Within five (5) years of the date of the veteran's release from active duty, five (5) preference credit points shall be added, upon request, to the final passing score in any eligible examination taken by the veteran.

(b) Without regard to time limitations, five (5) preference credit points shall be added, upon request, to the final passing score in any eligible examination taken by the surviving spouses of veterans.

(c) Without regard to time limitations, ten (10) preference credit points shall be added, upon request, to the final passing score in any eligible examination taken by disabled veterans, spouses of disabled veterans having greater than fifty (50) percent disability, surviving spouses of veterans having children under eighteen years of age, or surviving spouses of veterans with continued parental care of a handicapped child.

# MINNESOTA
## (Minnesota Statutes)

**Section 43A.11.** Veteran's preference

(1) Creation. Recognizing that training and experience in the military service of the government and loyalty and sacrifice for the government are qualifications of merit which cannot readily be assessed by examination. A veteran's preference shall be available pursuant to this section to a veteran as defined in section 197.447.

(2) Restrictions. Veteran's preference credit under this section may not be used by any veteran who is currently receiving or is eligible to receive a monthly veteran's pension based exclusively on the length of military service.

(3) Non-disabled veteran's credit. There shall be added to the competitive open examination rating of a non-disabled veteran who so elects, a credit of five points provided that the veteran obtained a passing rating on the examination without the addition of the credit points.

(4) Disabled veteran's credit. There shall be added to the competitive open examination rating of a disabled veteran who so elects, a credit of ten points provided that the veteran obtained a passing rating on the examination without the addition of the credit points. There shall be added to the competitive promotional examination rating of a disabled veteran who so elects, a credit of five points provided that (a) the veteran obtained a passing rating on the examination without the addition of the credit points and (b) the veteran is applying for a first promotion after securing public employment.

(5) Disabled veteran; definitions. For the purpose of the preference to be used in securing appointment from a competitive open examination, "disabled veteran" means a person who has a compensable service-connected disability as adjudicated by the United States Veterans Administration or by the retirement board of one of the several branches of the armed forces, which disability is existing at the time preference is claimed. For purposes of the preference to be used in securing appointment from a competitive promotional examination, "disabled veteran" means a person who, at the time of election to use a promotional preference, is entitled to disability compensation under laws administered by the Veterans Administration for a permanent service-connected disability rated at fifty (50) percent or more.

### Section 197.447. Veteran defined

The word "veteran" as used in Minnesota Statutes, except in sections 136C.13, 196.21, 197.971 and 243.251, means a citizen of these United States or a resident alien who has been separated under honorable conditions from any branch of the armed forces of the United States after having served on active duty for 181 consecutive days or by reason of disability incurred while serving on active duty, or who has active military service certified under section 401 of Public Law 95-202. The active military service must be certified by the U.S. Secretary of Defense as active military service and a discharge under honorable conditions must have been issued by the Secretary.

# MISSISSIPPI
## (Mississippi Code)

### Section 25-9-301. Definitions.

The following terms shall have the meaning ascribed herein unless the context shall require otherwise:

(a) "Veteran" means a person who served in the active armed forces of the United States for a period of ninety (90) days during a period of war or armed conflict and was granted an honorable discharge therefrom, or was discharged therefrom for a service-connected injury in less than ninety (90) days.

(b) "Disabled veteran" means a veteran who the Veterans Administration has certified to have a service-connected disability within the last ninety (90) days.

### Section 25-9-303. Preference for veterans in appointment, promotion and layoffs

(1) The state personnel board shall grant each veteran who is fully qualified preference over other applicants for an initial or promotional appointment. Disabled veterans shall be given additional preference.

(2) In establishing a layoff formula or procedure, the state personnel board shall grant preference to veterans and additional preference to disabled veterans.

## (Mississippi Personnel Regulations)

### Section 4.16. Award of veterans' preference points

The veteran status of an applicant may increase the numerical rating of the applicant. If the applicant attains a passing grade on an examination or is otherwise qualified to be placed on a list of eligibles, a total of five (5) points will be added to the final grade for veteran status, and a total of ten (10) points will be added for disabled veteran status. The final grade for an applicant is normally based on a one hundred (100) point scale. Scores of applicants awarded veterans' preference points may exceed the one hundred (100) point scale. Points shall not be awarded for periods of active duty when duty was for "training purposes only" to meet obligations in the reserve forces, National Guard, etc.

# MISSOURI
## (Missouri Statutes)

**Section 285.235.** Definitions

As used in sections 285.235 and 285.237, the following terms shall mean:

(1) "Armed forces of the United States," the army, air force, navy, marine corps, coast guard and any other military branch of service that is designated by Congress as a part of the Armed Forces of The United States;

(2) "Disabled veteran," a veteran who is entitled to, or who but for the receipt of military retirement pay would be entitled to, compensation under any law administered by the Department of Veterans Affairs and who is not a special disabled veteran;

(3) "Eligible veteran," a person who served on active duty for more than one hundred eighty days and was discharged or released from active duty with other than a dishonorable discharge, or a person who was discharged or released from active duty because of a service disability;

(4) "Employment program," (deleted)

(5) "Entitlement program," (deleted)

(6) "Other eligible person, one of the following:

(a) The spouse of any person who died of a service-connected disability;

(b) The spouse of any member of the armed forces serving on active duty who is at the time of the spouse's application for assistance under any program described in subsection 1 of section 285.237:

(1) missing in action

(2) captured in the line of duty by a hostile force

(3) forcibly detained or interned in the line of duty by a foreign government or power;

(c) The spouse of any person who has a total disability permanent in nature resulting from a service-connected disability, or the spouse of a veteran who died while such a disability was in existence;

(7) "Special disabled veteran," a veteran who is entitled to, or who but for the receipt of military pay would be entitled to, compensation under any law administered by the Department of Veterans Affairs for a disability rated at thirty percent or more, or a person who was discharged or released from active duty because of a service-connected disability;

(8) "Target-specific veterans," veterans who are:

(a) recently discharged veterans;

(b) minority veterans;

(c) veterans of the Vietnam Era;

(d) disabled veterans;

(9) "Targeted group," (deleted)

(10) "Training program," (deleted)

(11) "Veteran," any person who was a member of the armed forces of the United States for a period of one hundred eighty days or more or a person who was discharged or released from active duty because of a service-connected disability;

(12) "Veteran of the Vietnam Era," an eligible veteran who served on active duty for a period of more than one hundred eighty days, any part of which occurred from August 5, 1964 to May 7, 1975.

**Section 285.237.** Certain job openings and training priorities for veterans; annual report by state agencies; duties of certain state agencies

(1) Any federally funded employment and training program administered by any state agency, including but not limited to the Job Training Partnership Act, 29 U. S. C. 1501, shall include a veteran priority system to provide maximum employment and training opportunities to veterans and other eligible persons within each targeted group as established by federal law and state and federal policy in the service area. Disabled veterans, target- specific veterans groups, other veterans and other eligible persons shall receive preference over non-veterans within each targeted group in the provision of employment and training services available through these programs as required by this section.

(2) Each state agency shall refer qualified applicants to job openings and training opportunities in programs described in subsection 1 of this section in the following order of priority:

(1) Special disabled veterans;

(2) target specific veterans;

(3) all other veterans

(4) other eligible persons

(5) non-veterans

*Section 36.220.* Preference ratings for veterans

(1) In any competitive examination given for the purpose of establishing a register of eligibles, veterans, disabled veterans, surviving spouses and spouses of disabled veterans shall be given preference in appointment and examination in the following manner:

(a) A veteran or the surviving spouse of a veteran whose name appears on a register of eligibles who made a passing grade, shall have five points added to his or her final grade, and his or her rank on the register shall be determined on the basis of this augmented grade.

(b) The spouse of a disabled veteran whose name appears on a register of eligibles and who has made a passing grade, shall have five points added to his or her final grade, and his or her rank on the register shall be determined on the basis of this augmented grade. This preference shall be given only if the veteran is not employed in the state service and the disability renders him or her unqualified for entrance into the state service.

(c) A disabled veteran whose name appears on a register of eligibles and who made a passing grade shall have ten points added to his or her final grade, and his or her rank on the register shall be determined on the basis of this augmented grade.

(2) Any person who has been honorably discharged from the armed forces of the United States shall receive appropriate credit for any training and experience gained therein in any examination if the training or experience is related to the duties of the class of positions for which the examination is given.

# MONTANA
## (Montana Code)

**Section 39-29-101.** Definitions

For the purposes of this chapter, the following definitions apply:

(1) "Active duty" means full-time duty with military pay and allowances in the armed forces, except for training, determining physical fitness, or service in the reserve or National Guard.

(2) "Armed forces" means the United States:

(a) army, navy, air force, marine corps and coast guard; and

(b) merchant marine for service recognized by the U.S. Department of Defense as active military service for the purpose of laws administered by the Department of Veterans Affairs.

(3) "Disabled veteran" means a person:

(a) whether or not the person is a veteran as defined in this section, who was separated under honorable conditions from active duty in the armed forces and has established the present existence of a service-connected disability or is receiving compensation, disability retirement benefits or pension because of a law administered by the Department of Veterans Affairs or a military department; or

(b) who has received a Purple Heart medal.

(4) "Eligible relative" means:

(a) the unmarried surviving spouse of a veteran or disabled veteran;

(b) the spouse of a disabled veteran who is unable to qualify for an appointment to a position;

(c) the mother of a veteran who died under honorable conditions while serving in the armed forces if:

(1) the mother's spouse is totally and permanently disabled; or

(2) the mother is the widow of the father of the veteran and has not remarried;

(d) the mother of a service-connected permanently and totally disabled veteran if:

(1) the mother's spouse is totally and permanently disabled; or

(2) the mother is the widow of the father of the veteran and has not remarried.

(5) "Position" means a position occupied by a permanent, temporary or seasonal employee as defined in Sec. 2-18-101 for the state or similar permanent, temporary or seasonal employee with a public employer other than the state. This term does not include:

(a) a state or local elected office;

(b) appointment by an elected official to a body such as a board, commission, committee or council;

(c) appointment by an elected official to a public office if the appointment is provided for by law;

(d) a department head appointment by the governor or an executive department head appointment by a mayor, city manager, county commissioner or other chief administrative or executive officer of a local government; or

(e) engagement as an independent contractor or employment by an independent contractor.

(6) "Public employer" means:

(a) a department, office, board, bureau, commission, agency or other instrumentality of the executive, legislative or judicial branches of the government of this state;

(c) a unit of the Montana university system;

(d) a school district or community college; and

(e) a county, city or town.

(7) "Scored procedure" means a written test, structured oral interview, performance test or other selection procedure or a combination of these procedures that results in a numerical score to which percentage points may be added.

(7) "Under honorable conditions" means a discharge or separation from active duty characterized by the armed forces as under honorable conditions. The term includes honorable discharges and general discharges but does not include dishonorable discharges or other administrative discharges characterized as other than honorable.

(8) "Veteran" means a person who:

(a) was separated under honorable conditions from active duty in the armed forces after having served more than 180 consecutive days, other than for training; or

(b) as a member of a reserve component under an order of active duty pursuant to 10 U. S. C. 12301 (a),(d) or (g), 10 U. S. C. 12302, OR 10

U. S. C. 12304 served on active duty during a period of war or in a campaign or expedition for which a campaign badge is authorized and was discharged or released from duty under honorable conditions.

**Section 39-29-102.** Point preference in initial hiring for certain applicants

(1) Subject to the restrictions in subsections (2) and (3), whenever a public employer uses a scored procedure, an applicant for an initial hiring, as defined in 39-30-103, must have added to his score the following percentage points of the total possible points that may be granted in the scored procedure:

(a) five percentage points if the applicant is a veteran; and

(b) ten percentage points if the applicant is a disabled veteran or an eligible relative.

(2) A veteran, disabled veteran or eligible relative may not receive the percentage points provided for in subsection (1) unless the person;

(a) is a U.S. citizen; and

(b) received 70 or more percentage points of the total possible points that may be granted in the scored procedure.

(3) A disabled veteran who receives ten percentage points under subsection (1)(b) may not receive an additional five percentage points under subsection (1)(a).

**Section 39-29-103.** Notice and claim of preference

(1) A public employer shall, by posting or on the application form, give notice of the point preference provided in 39-29-102.

(3) A job applicant who believes that he is eligible to receive a point preference shall claim the preference in writing before the time for filing applications for the position involved has passed. Failure to make a timely preference claim for a position is a complete defense to an action instituted by an applicant under 39-29-104 with regard to that position.

(4) If an applicant for a position makes a timely written preference claim, the public employer shall give written notice of its hiring decision to the applicant claiming preference.

**Section 39-29-104.** Enforcement of preference.

(1) An applicant who believes that he is entitled to but has not been given the point preference provided for in 39-29-102 may, within 30 days

of receipt of the notice of the hiring decision provided for in 39-29-103, submit to the public employer a written request for an explanation of the public employer's hiring decision. Within fifteen days of receipt of the request, the public employer shall give the applicant a written explanation.

(2) After following the procedure described in subsection (1), the applicant may, within ninety days after receipt of the notice of the hiring decision, file a petition in the district court in the county in which his application was received by the public employer. The petition must state the facts that on their face entitle the applicant to a point preference.

# NEBRASKA
## (Nebraska Revised Statutes)

**Section 48-225.** Veterans preference; terms defined

As used in sections 48-225 to 48-231 unless the context requires a different meaning:

(1) "Veteran" shall mean any person who served on full-time active duty with military pay and allowances in the armed forces of the United States, except for training or for determining physical fitness, and was discharged therefrom under honorable conditions;

(2) "Full-time duty" shall mean duty during time of war or during a period recognized by the United States Department of Veterans Affairs as qualifying for veterans benefits administered by that department and that such duty from January 31, 1955 to August 5, 1964 shall have exceeded one hundred and eighty days unless lesser duty was the result of a service-connected or service-aggravated disability;

(3) "Disabled veteran" shall mean an individual who has served on active duty in the armed forces of the United States, has been separated therefrom under honorable conditions, and has established the present existence of a service-connected disability or is receiving compensation, disability retirement benefits or pension because of a public statute administered by the United States Department of Veterans Affairs or a military department; and

(4) "Preference eligible" shall mean any veteran as defined in this section.

**Section 48-226.** Veterans preference; required, when

A preference shall be given to preference eligibles seeking employment with the State of Nebraska or its governmental subdivisions in those agencies where there is no merit system in effect.

### Section 48-227. Veterans preference; examinations

A preference shall be given to preference eligibles seeking employment with the State of Nebraska or its governmental subdivisions in those agencies where there is a merit system in effect except as provided in section 48-228. Veterans who obtain passing scores on all parts or phases of an examination shall have five points added to their passing score if claim for such points is made on the application. An additional five points shall be added to the passing score of any disabled veteran.

### Section 48-228. Veterans preference; exceptions to act

The provisions of sections 48-225 to 48-231 and 55-161 shall not apply to any state agency or governmental subdivision subject to the Joint Merit System for the State of Nebraska.

# NEVADA
## (Nevada Revised Statutes)

### Section 284.253. Preference on list for residents of Nevada

In establishing lists of eligible persons, a preference must be allowed for persons who reside in this state at the time the examination is completed. Five points must be added to the passing grade achieved on the examination. For the purposes of this section, the person must reside physically within this state. If any person absents himself from this state with the intention in good faith to return without delay and continue his residence, the time of the absence must not be considered in determining the fact of his residence.

### Section 284.260. Veterans' preference; additional credits on examination

1. In establishing the lists of eligible persons, certain preferences must be allowed for veterans not dishonorably discharged from the armed forces of the United States. For disabled veterans, ten points must be added to the passing grade achieved on the examination. For ex-servicemen and

women who have not suffered disabilities, and for the widows and widowers of veterans, five points must be added to the passing grade achieved on the examination.

2. Any person qualifying for preference points pursuant to subsection 1 is entitled to have the points applied to any open competitive examination in the classified service but only to one promotional examination.

3. For the purposes of this section, "veteran" has the meaning ascribed to "eligible veteran" in 38 U.S.C. 4211.

# NEW HAMPSHIRE
## (New Hampshire Revised Statutes)

### Section 283.4. Employment of veterans

In public employment of clerks, office help, mechanics, laborers, inspectors, supervisors, foremen, janitors, peace officers and relief employees in the construction of public works, public projects and in the conduct of state, city, town or district departments by the state or by a county, city, town or district, or by persons contracting therewith for such construction, carrying out of relief projects and in the conduct of state, city, town or district departments, preference shall be given to citizens of this state who have served in the armed forces of the United States for not less than ninety days, in time of war, and have been discharged honorably therefrom or released from active duty therein, if qualified for said employment and if registered in accordance with the provisions of RSA 283.7. Where such employment is obtained from relief rolls or for persons in need, in cases of equal or greater need preference shall be given to veterans.

### Section 283.5. Widows of veterans; wives of disabled veterans

The employment preferences provided for veterans under the provisions of RSA 283.4 are extended to include any unremarried widow whose husband at the time of his death was a citizen of this state and who served in the armed forces of the United States during any war in which the United States has been engaged, and also to any wife of a totally disabled veteran who is a citizen of this state and who served in the armed forces of the United States during any war in which the United States has been engaged.

### Section 283.6. State and political subdivisions

The hiring authority of this state or any political subdivision thereof shall take any necessary action to secure the employment of said veterans in said service of this state or political subdivisions thereof respectively.

### Section 283.7. Proof of entitlement

Veterans, in order to be entitled to preference under this subdivision, shall furnish proof of such entitlement to the hiring authority of this state or political subdivision when applying for employment.

### (New Hampshire Personnel Regulations)

### Section 701.01. Seniority based on Full-time Employment

(a) Seniority shall be based on the length of continuous full-time employment with the state from the last date of hire.

(b) Full-time employment shall be calculated on the basis of years, months and days of service, except that any days, months or years of leave without pay for personal or educational purposes shall not be counted toward seniority.

(c) The length of seniority calculated under paragraph (b) shall include adjustments for prior military service as provided under section 701.02 and 701.03, except that any permanent employee who voluntarily leaves state service shall not be entitled to again receive a seniority adjustment for prior military service upon rehire.

### Section 701.02. Seniority Adjustments Due To Prior Military Service

(a) A permanent employee shall be granted seniority credit for each full month of verified service during a period of war or armed conflict as defined by section 701.02(b), as a result of a draft, enlistment period or federalization in the armed forces of the U.S., to a maximum of 12 months, provided:

(1) the employee has been honorably discharged or medically discharged under honorable circumstances; and

(2) the employee has filed proof of entitlement for adjustment due to prior military service

(b) To claim eligibility for seniority adjustment due to prior military service, the employee shall provide proof of active military service during a draft, enlistment period or federalization in the armed forces of the U.S. for the following eligibility dates:

(1) WWII between 7 Dec. 1941 and 31 Dec. 1946;

(2) Korean Conflict between 25 June 1950 and 31 Jan. 1955;

(3) Vietnam Conflict between 1 July 1958 and 22 Dec. 1961, if the employee earned the Vietnam service medal or the armed forces expeditionary medal;

(4) Vietnam Conflict between 22 Dec. 1961 and 7 May 1975; or

(5) Any other war or armed conflict that has occurred since 8 May 1975, and in which the employee earned an armed forces expeditionary medal or theater of operations service medal.

### Section 102.66. Veteran defined

A veteran is a person who has served not less than 90 days in active duty in the Armed Forces of the U.S. and who has been honorably discharged or medically discharged under honorable circumstances during a period of war, as set forth in section 701.02.

### Section 403.01. Register of eligible candidates

(c) The list of eligible candidates shall be arranged in descending order by examination score.

### Section 501.08. Examination procedures; veteran's preference

(a) To qualify for veteran's preference, the candidate shall establish, by presentation of an official record, that the veteran:

(1) has served not less than 90 days in the Armed Forces of the U.S. during a period of war, as defined by Section 701.02; and

(2) was honorably discharged or medically discharged under honorable conditions from such service.

(b) A candidate shall have 5 points added to any passing earned rating achieved in an examination for entrance to the state classified service if the candidate is:

(1) a qualifying veteran

(2) a spouse of a qualifying totally disabled veteran; or

(3) an unremarried surviving spouse of a qualifying veteran

(c) A candidate shall have 10 points added to any passing earned rating achieved in an examination for entrance to state classified service if the candidate is:

(1) a qualifying veteran with a service-connected disability rated by the DVA at 10 percent or more; or

(2) an unremarried spouse of a qualifying veteran whose death was service-connected.

# NEW JERSEY
## (New Jersey Statutes)

**Section 11A.5-1.** Definitions

As used in this chapter:

(a) "Disabled veteran" means any veteran who is eligible to be compensated for a service-connected disability from war service by the United States Veterans Administration or who receives or who is entitled to receive equivalent compensation for a service-connected disability which arises out of military or naval service as set forth in this chapter and who has submitted sufficient evidence of the record of disability incurred in the line of duty to the commissioner on or before the closing date for filing an application for an examination;

(b) "Veteran" means any honorably discharged soldier, sailor, marine or nurse who served in any army or navy of the allies of the United States in World War I, between July 14, 1914 and November 11, 1918, or who served in any army or navy of the allies of the United States between September 1, 1939 and September 2, 1945 and who was inducted into that service through voluntary enlistment, and was a citizen of these United States at the time of the enlistment, and who did not renounce or lose his or her U.S. citizenship; or any soldier, sailor, marine, airman, nurse or army field clerk who has served in the active military or naval service of the United States and has been discharged or released under other than dishonorable conditions from that service in any of the following wars or conflicts and who has presented to the commissioner sufficient evidence of the record of such service on or before the closing date for filing an application for an examination:

(1) World War I, between April 6, 1917 and November 11, 1918;

(2) World War II, on or after September 16, 1940, and who shall have served at least ninety days beginning on or before December 31, 1946 in such active service, exclusive of any period of assignment for a course of education or training under the Army Specialized Training Program or the Navy College Training Program, which course was a continuation of a civilian course and was pursued to completion, or as a cadet

or midshipman at one of the service academies; except that any person receiving an actual service-incurred injury or disability shall be classed a veteran whether or not that person has completed the ninety day service;

(3) Korean Conflict on or after June 23, 1950, who shall have served at least ninety days beginning on or before January 31, 1955, in active service, exclusive of any period of assignment for a course of education or training under the Army Specialized Training Program or the Navy College Training Program, which course was a continuation of a civilian course and was pursued to completion, or as a cadet or midshipman at one of the service academies; except that any person receiving an actual service-incurred injury or disability shall be classed a veteran, whether or not that person has completed the ninety day service;

(4) Vietnam Conflict, on or after December 31, 1960, who shall have served at least ninety days beginning on or before May 7, 1975, in active service, exclusive of any period of assignment for a course of education or training under the Army Specialized Training Program or the Navy College Training Program, which course was a continuation of a civilian course and was pursued to completion, or as a cadet or midshipman at one of the service academies, and exclusive of any service performed pursuant to the provisions of section 511 (d) of Title 10, U. S. C., or exclusive of any service performed pursuant to enlistment in the National Guard or the Army Reserve, Naval Reserve, Air Force Reserve, Marine Corps Reserve or Coast Guard Reserve; except that any person receiving an actual service-incurred injury or disability shall be classed a veteran, whether or not that person has completed the ninety day service as provided;

(5) Lebanon peacekeeping mission, on or after September 26, 1982, who has served in Lebanon or on board any ship actively engaged in patrolling the territorial waters of that nation for a period, continuous or in the aggregate, of at least fourteen days commencing on or before the date of termination of that mission, as proclaimed by the President of the United States, Congress or the Governor, whichever date of termination is the latest, in such active service; provided that any person receiving an actual service-incurred injury or disability shall be classed as a veteran whether or not that person has completed the fourteen days service as herein provided;

(6) Grenada peacekeeping mission, on or after October 25, 1983, who has served in Grenada or on board any ship actively engaged in

patrolling the territorial waters of that nation for a period, continuous or in the aggregate, of at least fourteen days commencing on or before the date of termination of that mission, as proclaimed by the President of the United States, Congress or the Governor, whichever date of termination is the latest, in such active service; provided that any person receiving an actual service-incurred injury or disability shall be classed as a veteran whether or not that person has completed the fourteen days service as herein provided;

(7) Panama peacekeeping mission, on or after the date of inception of that mission, as proclaimed by the President of the United States, Congress or the Governor, whichever date of inception is earliest, who has served in Panama or on board any ship actively engaged in patrolling the territorial waters of that nation for a period, continuous or in the aggregate, of at least fourteen days commencing on or before the date of termination of that mission, as proclaimed by the President of the United States, Congress or the Governor, whichever date of termination is the latest, in such active service; provided that any person receiving an actual service-incurred injury or disability shall be classed as a veteran whether or not that person has completed the fourteen days service as herein provided;

(8) Operation "Desert Shield/Desert Storm" mission in the Arabian Peninsula and in the Persian Gulf, on or after the date of inception of that operation, as proclaimed by the President of the United States, Congress or the Governor, whichever date of inception is earliest, who has served in the Arabian Peninsula or on board any ship actively engaged in patrolling the Persian Gulf for a period, continuous or in the aggregate, of at least fourteen days commencing on or before the date of termination of that mission, as proclaimed by the President of the United States, Congress or the Governor, whichever date of termination is the latest, in such active service; provided that any person receiving an actual service-incurred injury or disability shall be classed as a veteran whether or not that person has completed the fourteen days service as herein provided;

### Section 11A.5-4. Disabled veterans' preference

The names of disabled veterans who receive passing scores on open competitive examinations shall be placed at the top of the employment list in the order of their respective final scores.

### Section 11A.5-5. Veterans' preference

The names of veterans who receive passing scores on open competitive examinations shall be placed on the employment list in order of their respective final scores immediately after disabled veterans.

# NEW MEXICO
*(New Mexico Statutes)*

**Section 10-9-13.2.** Veteran's preference

A. In establishing a list of eligibles for appointment, the board shall provide preference points for veterans honorably discharged from the armed forces of the United States. Veterans with a service-connected disability shall be awarded ten points over and above their regular test scores. Veterans without a service-connected disability shall be awarded five points over and above their regular test scores.

B. The board shall determine the rank on any employment list by adding the points to the veteran's final passing grade on the examination after the veteran has submitted proof of having status as a veteran at the time of application for employment with a state agency. In the case of a veteran having a service-connected disability, the veteran shall provide proof of a service-connected disability in the form of a certification by the federal Veterans Administration. A veteran with or without a service-connected disability shall have his name placed on the list in accordance with the numerical rating of other veterans and non-veterans.

# NEW YORK
*(Consolidated Laws of New York)*

**Article VI, Section 85.** Additional credit allowed veterans in competitive examinations; preference in retention upon abolition of positions

(1) Definitions

(a) The terms "veteran" and "non-disabled veteran" mean a member of the armed forces of the United States who served therein in time of war, who was honorably discharged or released under honorable circumstances from such service, who was a resident of this state at the time of entrance into the armed forces of the United States and who is a citizen of these United States or an alien lawfully admitted for permanent residence in these United States at the time of application for appointment or promotion or at the time of retention, as the case may be.

(b) The term "disabled veteran" means a veteran who is certified by the United States Veterans Administration as entitled to receive disability payments upon the certification of such Veterans Administration for a disability incurred by him in time of war and in existence at the time of application for appointment or promotion or at the time of retention, as the case may be. Such disability shall be deemed to be in existence at the time of application for appointment or promotion or at the time of retention, as the case may be, if the certificate of such Veterans Administration shall state affirmatively that such veteran has been examined by a medical officer of such Veterans Administration on a date within one year of either the date of filing application for competitive examination for original appointment or promotion or the date of the establishment of the resulting eligible list, or within one year of the time of retention, as the case may be; that at the time of such examination the war-incurred disability described in such certificate was found to exist; and that such disability is rated at ten percentum or more. Such disability shall also be deemed to be in existence at such time if the certificate of such Veterans Administration shall state affirmatively that a permanent stabilized condition of disability exists to an extent of ten percentum or more, notwithstanding the fact that such veteran has not been examined by a medical officer of such Veterans Administration within one year of either the time of application for appointment or promotion or the date of filing application for competitive examination for original appointment or promotion, or within one year of the time of retention, as the case may be. The term "disabled veteran" shall also mean:

(1) A veteran who served in World War I, who continued to serve in the armed forces of the United States after November 11, 1918, and who is certified, as hereinbefore provided, by the U.S. Veterans Administration as receiving disability payments upon the certification of such Veterans Administration for a disability incurred by him in such service on or before July 2, 1921.

(2) A veteran who served in World War II, who continued to serve in the armed forces of the United States after September 2, 1945, and who is certified, as hereinbefore provided, by the U.S. Veterans Administration as receiving disability payments upon the certification of such Veterans Administration for a disability incurred by him

in such service on or before the date that World War II is declared terminated.

(3) A veteran who served during hostilities participated in by the military forces of the United States subsequent to June 25, 1950, who continued to serve in the armed forces of the United States after July 27, 1953, and who is certified, as hereinbefore provided, by the U.S. Veterans Administration as receiving disability payments upon the certification of such Veterans Administration for a disability incurred by him in such service on or before the date that the Korean Conflict is declared terminated.

(c) The term "time of war" shall include the following wars for the periods herein set forth:

(1) World War I, from April 6, 1917 to and including November 11, 1918;

(2) World War II, from December 7, 1941 to and including September 2, 1945;

(3) Hostilities participated in by the military forces of the United States from June 26, 1950 to and including January 31, 1955;

(4) Hostilities participated in by the military forces of the United States from January 1, 1963 to March 29, 1973.

(d) The term "application for original appointment or promotion" shall mean the date of the establishment of an eligible list resulting from a competitive examination for original appointment or promotion, as the case may be, which date shall be the date on which the term of such eligible list commences.

(e) The term "time of retention" shall mean the time of abolition or elimination of positions.

(2) Additional credits in competitive examinations for original appointment or promotion:

(a) On all eligible lists resulting from competitive examinations, the names of eligibles shall be entered in the order of their respective final earned ratings on the examination, with the name of the eligible with the highest final earned rating at the head of such list, provided however that for the purpose of determining final earned ratings:

(1) Disabled veterans shall be entitled to receive ten points additional in a competitive examination for original appointment and five points additional credit in a competitive examination for promotion; and

(2) Non-disabled veterans shall be entitled to receive five points additional credit in a competitive examination for original appointment and two and one-half points additional credit in a competitive examination for promotion.

(b) Such additional credit shall be added to the final earned rating of such disabled veteran or non-disabled veteran, as the case may be, after he or she has qualified in the competitive examination and shall be granted only at the establishment of the resulting eligible list.

4. Application for additional credit; proof of eligibility; establishment of eligible list. Any candidate, believing himself entitled to additional credit in a competitive examination as provided herein, may make application for such additional credit at any time between the date of his application for examination and the date of the establishment of the resulting eligible list. Such candidates shall be allowed a period of not less than two months from the date of filing of his application for examination in which to establish by appropriate documentary proof his eligibility to receive additional credit under this section. At any time after two months have elapsed since the final date for filing applications for a competitive examination for original appointment or promotion, the eligible list resulting from such examination may be established, notwithstanding the fact that a veteran or disabled veteran who has applied for additional credit has failed to establish his eligibility to receive such additional credit. A candidate who fails to establish, by appropriate documentary proof, his eligibility to receive additional credit by the time an eligible list is established shall not thereafter be granted additional credit on such eligible list.

5. Use of additional credit. (a) Except as herein otherwise provided, no person who has received a permanent original appointment or a permanent promotion in the civil service of the state or of any city or civil division thereof from an eligible list on which he was allowed the additional credit granted by this section, either as a veteran or as a disabled veteran, shall thereafter be entitled to any additional credit under this section either as a veteran or as a disabled veteran.

(c) Where, at the time of the establishment of an eligible list, the position of a veteran or a disabled veteran on such list has not been affected by the addition of credits granted under this section, the appointment or promotion of such veteran or disabled veteran, as the case may be, from such eligible list shall not be deemed to have been made from an eligible list on which he was allowed the additional credit granted by this section.

(d) If, at the time of appointment from an eligible list, a veteran or disabled veteran is in the same relative standing among the eligibles who are willing to accept appointment as if he had not been granted the additional credits provided by this section, his appointment from among such eligibles shall not be deemed to have been made from an eligible list on which he was allowed such additional credits.

(e) Where a veteran or disabled veteran has been originally appointed or promoted from an eligible list on which he was allowed additional credit, but such appointment or promotion is thereafter terminated at the end of a probationary term or by resignation at or before the end of the probationary term, he shall not be deemed to have been appointed or promoted, as the case may be, from an eligible list on which he was allowed additional credit, and such appointment or promotion shall not affect his eligibility for additional credit in other examinations.

6. Withdrawal of application; election to relinquish additional credit. An application for additional credit in a competitive examination under this section may be withdrawn by the applicant at any time prior to the establishment of the resulting eligible list. At any time during the term of existence of an eligible list resulting from a competitive examination in which a veteran or disabled veteran has received the additional credit granted by this section, such veteran or disabled veteran may elect, prior to permanent original appointment or permanent promotion, to relinquish the additional credit theretofore granted to him and accept the lower position on such eligible list to which he would otherwise have been entitled; provided however, that such election shall thereafter be irrevocable. Such election shall be in writing and signed by the veteran or disabled veteran, and transmitted to the state civil service department or the appropriate municipal civil service commission.

7. Roster. The state civil service department and each municipal commission shall establish and maintain in its office a roster of all veterans and disabled veterans appointed or promoted as a result of additional credits granted by this section to positions under its jurisdiction. The appointment or promotion of a veteran or disabled veteran as a result of additional credits shall be void if such veteran or disabled veteran, prior to such appointment or promotion, had been appointed or promoted as a result of additional credits granted by this section.

8. Preference in retention upon the abolition of positions. In the event of abolition or elimination of any position in the civil service for which eligible lists are established or any position the incumbent of which is encompassed by section 80 (a) of this chapter, any suspension, demotion or displacement shall be made in the inverse order of the date of the original appointment in the service, subject to the following conditions: (1) blind employees shall be granted absolute preference in retention; (2) the date of such original appointment for disabled veterans shall be deemed to be 60 months earlier than the actual date, determined in accordance with section 30 of the general construction law; (3) the date of such original appointment for non-disabled veterans shall be deemed to be 30 months earlier than the actual date, determined in accordance with section 30 of the general construction law; (4) no permanent competitive class employee subject to the jurisdiction of the civil service commission of the City of New York who receives an injury in the line of duty, as defined in this paragraph, which requires immediate hospitalization, and which is not compensable through workmen's compensation may be suspended, demoted or displaced pursuant to section 80 of this chapter within three months of the date of his confinement, provided that medical authorities approved by such commission shall certify that such employee is not able to perform the duties of his position; provided further that such three-month period may be extended by such commission for additional periods not to exceed one year each upon the certification of medical authorities selected by such commission that the employee is, as a result of his injury, still not able to perform the duties of his position. An injury in the line of duty, as used herein, shall be construed to mean an injury which is incurred as a direct result of the lawful performance of the duties of the position. In determining whether an injury was received in the line of duty, such commission shall require the head of the agency by which the employee is employed to certify that the injury was received as a direct result of the lawful performance of the employee's duties, and (5) the spouse of a veteran with a one hundred percent service-connected disability shall be deemed to be 60 months earlier than the actual date, determined in accordance with section 30 of the general construction law, provided that the spouse is domiciled with the veteran-spouse and is the head of the household. This section shall not be construed as conferring any additional benefit upon such employee other than a preference in retention. Such employee shall be subject

to transfer upon the abolition of his function within his agency or department.

# NORTH CAROLINA
## (North Carolina General Statutes)

### Article 13. Veteran's Preference

*Section 126-80.* Declaration of policy

It shall be the policy of the State of North Carolina that, in appreciation for their service to this state and to this country during a period of war, and in recognition of the time and advantage lost toward the pursuit of a civilian career, veterans shall be granted preference in employment for positions subject to the provisions of this chapter with every state department, agency and institution.

*Section 126-81.* Definitions

As used in this article:

(1) "A period of war" includes World War I (April 6, 1917 through November 11, 1918), World War II (December 7, 1941 through December 31, 1946), the Korean Conflict (June 27, 1950 through January 31, 1955), and the end of the hostilities in Vietnam (May 7, 1975), or any other campaign, expedition or engagement for which a campaign badge or medal is authorized by the United States Department of Defense.

(2) "Veteran" means a person who served in the armed forces of the United States on active duty, for reasons other than training, and has been discharged under other than dishonorable conditions.

(3) "Eligible veteran" means:

(a) a veteran who served during a period of war; or

(b) the spouse of a disabled veteran; or

(c) the surviving spouse or dependent of a veteran who died on active duty during a period of war either directly or indirectly as a result of such service; or

(d) a veteran who suffered a service-connected disability during peacetime; or

(e) the spouse of a veteran described in subdivision (d) of this subsection; or

(f) the surviving spouse or dependent of a person who served in the armed forces of the United States on active duty, for reasons other than training, who died for service-related reasons during peacetime.

**Section 126-82.** State Personnel Commission to provide for preference

(a) The State Personnel Commission shall provide that in evaluating the qualifications of an eligible veteran against the minimum requirements for obtaining a position, credit shall be given for all military service training or schooling and experience that bears a reasonable and functional relationship to the knowledge, skills and abilities required for the position.

(b) The State Personnel Commission shall provide that if an eligible veteran has met the minimum requirements for the position, after receiving experience credit under subsection (a) of this section, he shall receive experience credit as determined by the Commission for additional related and unrelated military service.

(c) The State Personnel Commission may provide that in reduction in force situations where seniority or years of service is one of the considerations for retention, an eligible veteran shall be accorded credit for military service.

(d) Any eligible veteran who has reason to believe that he or she did not receive a veteran's preference in accordance with the provisions of this article or rules adopted under it may appeal directly to the State Personnel Commission.

(e) The willful failure of any employee subject to the provisions of Article 8 of this chapter to comply with the provisions of this article or rules adopted under it constitutes personal misconduct in accordance with the provisions and promulgated rules of this chapter, including those for suspension, demotion or dismissal.

*(North Carolina Personnel Manual)*

**Section 3.** Recruitment and selection (excerpts)

Included periods of military service:
- December 7, 1941 through May 15, 1975
- June 6, 1983 through December 1, 1987
- December 20, 1989 through January 31, 1990

- August 2, 1990 through the date approved by Congress or the President as the ending date for hostilities for the Persian Gulf War

Excluded periods of military service:

- May 16, 1975 through May 31, 1983
- December 2, 1987 through December 19, 1989
- February 1, 1990 through August 1, 1990

## Minimum Qualifications

In evaluating qualifications of qualified veterans, credit shall be given on a year for year, and month for month basis, for all military service training and experience which bears a reasonable functional relationship to the knowledge, skills and abilities required for the position applied for.

Advisory note: In determining minimum education and experience, related civilian experience should be used prior to using related military experience, in order to give the veteran the maximum credit for unrelated military service.

## Determining Military Service Credit

In initial selection procedures, where numerically scored examinations are used in determining the relative ranking of candidates, ten (10) preference points shall be awarded to eligible veterans.

In initial selection, where structured interview, assessment center, in-basket, or any other procedure, not numerically scored, is used to qualitatively assess the relative ranking of candidates, the veteran who has met the minimum qualification requirements and who has less than four years of related military experience beyond that necessary to minimally qualify, shall also receive additional experience credit for up to four years of unrelated military service.

The amount of additional experience credit to be granted for unrelated military service in individual cases shall be determined as follows:

Determine the amount of related military service possessed by the eligible veteran beyond that required to meet the minimum qualifications and:

- if the total of such experience equals or exceeds four years, the additional credit for unrelated military service does not apply, but

- if the total of such experience is less than four years, the veteran shall receive direct experience credit for unrelated military service in an amount not to exceed the difference between the related military service and the four-year maximum credit which may be granted.

## Applying preference

After applying the preference, the qualified eligible veteran shall be hired when overall qualifications are substantially equal to one or more non-veterans or non-eligible veterans in the applicant pool. Substantially equal qualifications occur when the employer cannot make a reasonable determination that the qualifications held by one or more persons are significantly better suited for the position than the qualifications held by another person.

In reduction-in-force situations where seniority or years of service is one of the considerations in retention, the eligible veteran shall be accorded one year of state service for each year or fraction thereof of military service, up to a maximum of five (5) years credit.

## Relationship to other priorities

If the selection decision is between a qualified non-state employee veteran and a substantially equivalent applicant with a priority described below, the applicant with the priority described below shall be selected:

- a qualified current state employee with career status who is seeking a promotional opportunity,

- a qualified employee separated from policy-making confidential exempt job for reasons other than just cause,

- a qualified state employee notified of or separated by reduction-in-force, or

- an employee returning from workers' compensation leave.

# NORTH DAKOTA
### (North Dakota Century Code)

**Section 37-01-40.** "Veteran" and "wartime veteran" defined; uniform service dates for wartime veterans

(1) A "veteran" is a person who has served on continuous federalized active military duty for twenty-four months or the full period for which the person was called or ordered to active military duty, whichever is shorter, and who was discharged or released therefrom under other than dishonorable conditions. A discharge reflecting "expiration of term of service" or "completion of required service," or words to that effect qualifies the shorter term of service as making the person a veteran.

(2) A "wartime veteran" is a person who served in the active military forces during a period of war or who received the armed forces expeditionary or other campaign service medal during an emergency condition and who was discharged or released therefrom under other than dishonorable conditions. "Wartime veteran" also includes a person who died in the line of duty in the active military forces, as determined by the armed forces.

(3) In order to provide for the uniformity of period of service dates for wartime veterans, the following dates and terms are applicable to all acts of the state relative to wartime veterans where not otherwise specifically prescribed by statute:

(a) Civil War and Confederate veterans who served between April 12, 1861 and May 26, 1865;

(b) Future dates. The period beginning on the date of any future declaration of war by the Congress of the United States or the beginning of an emergency condition recognized by the issuance of a presidential proclamation or executive order and in which the armed forces expeditionary medal or other campaign service medals are awarded according to presidential executive order and ending on a date prescribed by presidential proclamation or concurrent resolution of the Congress of the United States.

(c) Indian Wars. Since the Indian Wars were fought intermittently over a period of years, the determination as to whether a person shall be considered as having rendered military service during these wars will be carefully considered by the administrative committee on Veterans' Affairs. January 1, 1817 through December 31, 1898 is considered the Indian War Period.

(d) "Korean Conflict" means the period between June 27, 1950 to January 31, 1955.

(e) Mexican Wars. Since there were several skirmishes involving the Mexican Border, such as the Mexican border troubles 1911–1916; Veracruz expedition April 21, 1914 to November 26, 1914; punitive expedition into Mexico, March 15, 1916 to February 5, 1917; therefore these persons rendering military service in any of these skirmishes must be considered veterans of the Mexican Wars between 1911 and February 5, 1917.

(f) "Spanish-American War" means the period beginning on April 21, 1898 and ending on July 4, 1902; includes the Philippine Insurrection and the Boxer Rebellion; and in the case of a veteran who served with the United States military forces engaged in hostilities in the Moro Province, means the period beginning on April 21, 1898 and ending on July 15, 1903.

(g) "Vietnam Era" means the period beginning August 5, 1964 and ending on May 7, 1975.

(h) "World War I" means the period beginning on April 6, 1917 and ending on November 11, 1918; and in the case of a veteran who served with the United States military forces in Russia, means the period beginning on April 6, 1917 and ending on April 1, 1920.

(i) "World War II" means the period beginning on December 7, 1941 and ending December 31, 1946, both dates inclusive.

### Section 37-19.1-01. Definitions

As used in this chapter:

(1) "Agency" or "governmental agency" means all political subdivisions and any state agency, board, bureau, commission, department, officer, and any state institution or enterprise authorized to employ persons either temporarily or permanently.

(2) "Disabled veteran" means a veteran who is found to be entitled to a service-connected disability rating as determined by the U.S. Veterans Administration.

(3) "Personnel system" means a personnel system based on merit principles.

(4) "Political subdivision" means counties, cities, townships and any other governmental entity created by state law which employs persons either temporarily or permanently.

(5) "Veteran:" means a wartime veteran as defined in subsection 2 of section 37-10-40.

### Section 37-19.1-02. Public employment preference for veterans; residency requirements

(1) Veterans who are North Dakota residents are entitled to preference, over all other applicants, in appointment or employment by governmental agencies, provided that such veteran is a United States citizen at the time of application for employment. Veterans qualified for preference may not be disqualified from holding any position with an agency because of mental or physical disability, unless such disability renders them unable to properly perform the duties of the position applied for.

(2) When a veteran applies for appointment or employment under subsection (1), the officer, board or person whose duty it is to appoint or employ a person to fill the available position shall, except where the veteran has been qualified for the position applied for under a personnel system, investigate the qualifications of the veteran. If the veteran is found to possess the qualifications required for the position applied for, whether educational or by way of prior experience, and is physically and mentally able to perform the duties of the position applied for, the officer, board or person shall appoint or employ the veteran.

(3) A disabled veteran is entitled to a preference superior to that given other veterans under this section, which preference must be accorded in the manner provided in this section.

(4) Notwithstanding the preference provisions in subsections (1), (2) and (3), public employment preferences for veterans by agencies or governmental agencies, as defined herein, which now have, or which may hereafter have, an established personnel system under which it maintains a register of persons eligible for employment and from which it certifies a prescribed number of names to that particular agency or governmental agency, must be governed by the following:

(a) No distinction or discrimination may be made in the administration of the examination because the applicant may be a veteran.

(b) Upon completion of the examination with a passing grade, the applicant must be informed of a veteran's rights to employment preference as hereinafter provided.

(c) The applicant must be required to furnish proof of his status as a veteran and, if disabled, proof of his disability, as defined herein.

(d) Upon receipt of proof required in subdivision (c), the examiner shall add five points for a non-disabled veteran and ten points for a disabled veteran to the examination grade of the applicant, and the total is the veteran's examination grade.

(e) Upon request for the prescribed number of eligible persons from the eligibility registry, such number of eligible persons must be certified from the top number of eligible persons and with such certified list of eligible persons there must also be submitted a statement as to which of those so certified are veterans, disabled veterans or non-veterans.

(f) In the event the certified list of eligible persons includes either veterans or disabled veterans, the appointing or employing authority of that particular agency or governmental agency shall make a selection for the available position as follows:

(1) A disabled veteran, without regard to his examination grade, is first entitled to the position and, in the absence of justifiable cause, documented in writing, for not making such selection, must be so appointed or employed. If such list includes two or more disabled veterans, then the one with the highest examination grade is first entitled to the position and, in the absence of justifiable cause, documented in writing, for not making such selection, must be so appointed or employed.

(2) When such certified list of eligible persons does not include one or more disabled veterans and consists only of veterans, then the one with the highest examination grade is first entitled to the position and, in the absence of justifiable cause, documented in writing, must be so appointed or employed.

(3) When such certified list of eligible persons includes non-veterans and veterans, but not disabled veterans, then the one with the highest examination grade, whether a non-veteran or a veteran, is first entitled to the position and, in the absence of justifiable cause, documented in writing, must be so appointed or employed; and if the one with the highest examination grade is a veteran and is not appointed or employed, there must be justifiable cause documented in writing for not making such appointment or employment.

(4) The provisions of this section do not apply when the position to be filled is that of a superintendent of schools, teacher, or the chief deputy or private secretary of an elected or appointed official. Temporary committees and individual or group appointments made by the governor or legislative assembly are also excepted from the provisions of this section.

Section 37-19.1-03. Preferences to be granted veterans' spouses

(1) The unremarried spouse of a veteran who died while in service, or later died from a service-connected cause or causes, is entitled, if he is otherwise qualified, to the appointment or employment preference given to a veteran under section 37-19.1-02 in the manner provided therein.

(2) The spouse of a disabled veteran, who is disabled due to a service-connected cause or causes, is, if the disabled veteran is unable to exercise his right to a veteran's employment preference due to his disability, entitled, if he is otherwise qualified, to the appointment or employment preference given to a veteran under section 37-19.1-02 in the manner provided therein.

# OHIO
## (Ohio Revised Code)

**Section 124.23.** Examinations; preferences; seniority

All applicants for positions and places in the classified service shall be subject to examination, except for applicants for positions in the professional or certified service and paraprofessional employees of county boards of mental retardation and developmental disabilities, who shall be hired in the manner provided in section 124.241 of the Revised Code.

Any examination administered under this section shall be public and open to all citizens of the United States and to those persons who have legally declared their intentions of becoming U.S. citizens, within certain limitations to be determined by the director of administrative services, as to citizenship, residence, age, experience, education, health, habit and moral character; provided any soldier, sailor, marine, coast guardsman, member of the auxiliary corps as established by Congress, member of the army nurse corps or the navy nurse corps; or red cross nurse who has served in the army, navy, or hospital service of the United States, and such other military service as is designated by Congress, including World War I, World War II, or during the period beginning May 1, 1949 and lasting so long as the armed forces of the United States are engaged in armed conflict or occupation duty, or the selective service or similar conscriptive acts are in effect in the United States, whichever is the later date, who has been honorably discharged therefrom or transferred to the reserve with evidence of satisfactory service, and is a resident of Ohio, may file with the director a certificate of service or honorable discharge, whereupon he shall receive additional credit of twenty percent of his total grade given in the regular examination in which he receives a passing grade. Such examination may include an evaluation of such factors as education, training, capacity, knowledge, manual dexterity, and physical or psychological fitness. Examinations shall consist of one or more tests in any combination. Tests may be written, oral, physical, demonstrations of skill, or an evaluation of training and experience and shall be designed to fairly test the relative capacity of the person examined to discharge the particular duties of the position for which appointment is sought. Where minimum or maximum requirements are established for any examination, they shall be specified in the examination announcement.

The director shall have control of all examinations, except as otherwise provided in sections 124.01 to 124.64 of the Revised Code. No questions in any examination shall relate to political or religious opinions or affiliations.

No credit for seniority, efficiency, or any other reason shall be added to an applicant's examination grade unless the applicant achieves at least the minimum passing grade on the examination without counting such extra credit.

Reasonable notice of the time, place and general scope of every competitive examination for appointment to a position in the civil service, except as otherwise provided in such sections, shall be given by the director. Written or printed notices of every examination of the state classified service shall be sent by the director to the clerk of the Court of Common Pleas of each county, and to the clerk of each city of the state, and such notices, promptly upon receipt, shall be posted in conspicuous public places, in the courthouse of the county, and in the city hall of the city. Such notices shall be posted in a conspicuous place in the office of the director for at least two weeks before any examination. In the case of examinations limited by the director to a district, county, or city, the director shall provide in his rules for adequate publicity of such examinations in the district, county or city within which competition is permitted.

Section 124.26. Eligible lists; veteran's preference

(A) Except as provided in divisions (B) and (C) of this section, from the returns of the examinations the director of administrative services shall prepare an eligible list of the persons whose general average standing upon examinations for such grade or class is not less than the minimum fixed by the rules of the director, and who are otherwise eligible; and such persons shall take rank upon the eligible list as candidates in the order of their relative excellence as determined by the examination. In the event two or more applicants receive the same mark in an open competitive examination, priority in the time of filing the application with the director shall determine the order in which their name shall be placed on the eligible list; provided, that applicants eligible for veteran's preference under section 124.23 of the Revised Code shall receive priority in rank on the eligible list over non-veterans on the list with a rating equal to that of the veteran. Ties among veterans shall be decided by the priority of filing the application. In the event of two or more applicants receiving the same mark on a promotional examination, seniority shall determine the order in which their names shall be placed on the eligible list. The term of eligibility of each list shall be fixed by the director at not less than one nor more than two years. When an eligible list is reduced to three names or less, a new list may be prepared. The director may consolidate two or more eligible lists of the same kind by the rearranging of eligibles therein, according to their grades.

(B) A person serving as a provisional employee who completes at least six months of service or his probationary period, whichever is longer, and passes an examination for the class or grade in which he holds his position shall be appointed as a permanent employee in the position before the director of administrative services prepares an eligible list.

*Section 124.27.* Appointments; certified and provisional; probationary period

Every soldier, sailor, marine, coast guardsman, member of the auxiliary corps as established by Congress, member of the army nurse corps, or navy nurse corps, or Red Cross nurse who has served in the army, navy, or hospital service of the United States, and such other military service as is designated by the Congress in the war with Spain, including the Philippine Insurrection and the China Relief Expedition, or from April 21, 1898 to July 4, 1902; World War I, World War II; or during the period beginning May 1, 1949 and lasting so long as the armed forces of the U.S. are engaged in armed conflict or occupation duty, or the selective service or similar conscriptive acts are in effect in the U.S., whichever is the later date, who has been honorably discharged or separated under honorable conditions therefrom, and is a resident of Ohio, and whose name is on an eligible list for a position, shall be entitled to preference in original appointments to any such competitive position in the civil service of this state and the civil divisions thereof, over all persons eligible for such appointments and standing on the list therefor, with a rating equal to that of each such person. Appointments to all such positions in the classified service that are not filled by promotion, transfer, or reduction as provided in sections 124.01 to 124.64 of the Revised Code, and the rules of the director prescribed under such sections, shall be made only from those persons whose names are certified to the appointing authority, and no employment, except as provided in such sections, shall be otherwise given in the classified service of this state or any political subdivision thereof.

# OKLAHOMA
## *(Oklahoma Statutes)*

**Title 72, Section 67.13(a). War veterans defined; retirement benefits**

The words "war veterans" used in this title shall be construed to mean such honorably discharged persons as:

(a) served in the Armed Forces of The United States at any time during the period from April 6, 1917 to November 11, 1918, both dates inclusive, or

(b) served in the armed forces of the U.S. as members of the 45th Division at any time during the period from September 16, 1940 to December 7, 1941 both dates inclusive, or

(c) served in the armed forces of the U.S. at any time during the period from December 7, 1941 to December 31, 1946, both dates inclusive, or

(d) served in the armed forces of the U.S. at any time during the period from June 27, 1950 to January 31, 1955, both dates inclusive, or

(e) served for a period of ninety days or more, unless discharged from active duty for a service-connected disability, in the armed forces of the U.S. during the period of time in which the U.S. participated in a war, campaign or battle, but excluding any person who shall have served on active duty for training only, unless discharged from active duty for service-connected disability, or

(f) served in the armed forces of the U.S. in a combat zone or in the immediate supporting area of the combat zone as certified by the War Veterans Commission of Oklahoma, prior to 5 August 1964, or

(g) served in the armed forces of the U.S. at any time during the period which began on 5 August 1964 and ended on 7 May 1975; except that such period shall be deemed to have ended on December 31, 1976, when determining eligibility for education and training benefits, or

(h) served in the armed forces of the U.S. at any time during the period which began on August 1, 1990 and ended on December 31, 1991, excluding any person who shall have served on active duty for training only, unless discharged from active duty for service-connected disability.

The term "war veterans" shall include only those persons who shall have served during the times or in the areas prescribed herein above, and those persons who were awarded service medals, as authorized by the U.S. Department of Defense as reflected in the veteran's Form DD 214, related to the Vietnam Conflict who served prior to 5 August 1964. Any honorably discharged war veteran of any of the armed forces of the U.S. shall be entitled to such tax exemptions to include but not be limited to tax-exempt veterans' benefits as provided in subsection (1), Section 2405 of Title 68 of the Oklahoma Statutes, special permits and veterans' preferences for state employment, provided, that any person who shall have served on active duty for training purposes only shall not be entitled to such tax exemptions, special permits or veterans' preferences.

War veterans, as defined above, shall receive maximum benefits available for each year of creditable service, not to exceed five years, for active military service for retirement benefits in the retirement systems within the State of Oklahoma; however, this provision shall apply to the Oklahoma Employment Security Commission only if approved by the federal funding source of the Oklahoma Employment Security Commission. The provisions of this act shall include military retirees whose retirement was based only on active service, that have been rated as having twenty percent or greater service-connected disability by the Veterans Administration of the Armed Forces of the U.S.

*Section 67.13(b).* Benefits for persons serving after January 31, 1955

Any person who served on active duty in the armed forces of the United States and was discharged or separated from active duty under conditions other than dishonorable and further had served such active duty for more than ninety days, other than for training purposes, any part of which occurred after January 31, 1955, or was released from active duty after January 31, 1955 for a service-connected disability, shall be entitled to tax exemptions, fees, special permits and veterans' preferences for state employment on the same basis as "war veterans" except as provided in Section 840.15 of Title 74 of the Oklahoma Statutes.

## Title 74, Section 840-4.12

Agencies of this state may use the optional hiring procedure provided in this section to employ females, blacks, Hispanics, Asian/Pacific Islanders and American Indian/Alaskan Natives, as defined by the Equal Employment Opportunity Commission, who are legal residents of this state in competitive and non-competitive jobs. Individuals must meet the minimum qualifications and pass any required examinations established by the Office of Personnel Management or by statute. Except for any required examinations and minimum qualifications specified in applicable job specifications, such persons shall be exempt from the hiring procedures administered by the Office of Personnel Management. Persons may only be employed under this subsection in a job class, group or category which has been identified as underutilized and in which an appropriate hiring goal has been set in the state agency's affirmative action plan approved by the Office of Personnel Management pursuant to the provisions of Section 840.25 of this title. In addition, the appointing authority of the employing agency must determine that a manifest imbalance exists which justifies remedial action pursuant to this subsection in order to reach the affirmative action hiring goal. Provided further, that eligible war veterans, as defined by Section 67.13 (a) of Title 72 of the Oklahoma Statutes, who are members of the group for which a hiring goal has been set shall be considered by the employing agency before a non-veteran is appointed pursuant to this subsection.

### Section 840-4.14. Preferences

A. In establishing employment lists of eligible persons for competitive and non-competitive appointment, certain preference shall be allowed for honorably discharged veterans as defined by Section 67.13(a) and Section 67.13(b) of Title 72 of the Oklahoma Statutes. In determination of the register rank:

(1) Five points shall be added to the final grade of any person who has passed the examination and has submitted proof of having status as a veteran or unremarried surviving spouse of a veteran;

(2) Five points shall be added to the final grade of any person who has passed the examination and has submitted proof of having status as a spouse of a veteran who is unemployable due to a service-connected disability as certified by the Veterans Administration or agency of the Defense Department within six months of the date of application; and

(3) Ten points shall be added to the final grade of any war veteran as defined in Section 67.13(a) of Title 72 of the Oklahoma Statutes who has passed the examination and has submitted proof of having a service-connected disability as certified by the Veterans Administration or agency of the Department of Defense within six months of date of application. Such veterans' names shall be placed at the top of the register in accordance with their numerical rating if in receipt of benefits payable at the rate of thirty percent (30%) or more and such veteran shall not be denied employment and passed over for other veterans or non-veterans without showing cause. Acceptable cause shall include a reasonable expectation of the inability of the preferenced applicant to satisfactorily perform at the required level of the position and shall be reviewed in each instance by the Administrator of the Office of Personnel Management. If the Administrator finds that acceptable cause for the denial of employment to the preferenced applicant does not exist, the appointing authority shall be required to hire the preferenced applicant. The position shall not be permanently filled until the Administrator has issued his findings.

B. War veterans, as defined by Section 67.13(a) of Title 72 of the Oklahoma Statutes, who have been awarded the Purple Heart or have a service-connected disability rated by the Veterans Administration or a branch of the armed forces of the U.S. and who have been a resident of Oklahoma for at least one year prior to the date of the examination, shall be authorized to open any closed register established by the Merit System of Personnel Administration.

C. Subsection A of this section shall not apply to special disabled veterans who are considered for employment under the provisions of Sections 401 through 404 of Title 72. Provided, said veterans may elect instead to be considered for employment according to the procedures set out in this section.

# OREGON
## (Oregon Revised Statutes)

### Section 408.225. Definitions

As used in ORS 408.225 TO 408.235:

(1) "Veteran" means a person, other than a person entitled to retirement pay from the United States based on length of military service, who served on active duty with the armed forces of the U.S. for a period of more than 180 consecutive days, and was discharged or released therefrom with other than a dishonorable discharge; or a person who served on active duty with the armed forces of the U.S. for 180 days or less and was discharged or released therefrom with other than a dishonorable discharge because of a service-connected disability. Attendance at a school under military orders, except schooling incident to an active enlistment or regular tour of duty, or normal military training as a reserve officer or member of an organized reserve or national guard unit shall not be considered active duty.

(2) "Disabled veteran" means a person entitled to disability compensation under laws administered by the U.S. Department of Veterans Affairs, a person whose discharge or release from active duty was for a disability incurred or aggravated in the line of duty, or a person who was awarded the Purple Heart for wounds received in combat.

### Section 408.230. Veterans' preference on civil service examinations

Every veteran and disabled veteran who has successfully completed all phases of a civil service test shall be allowed preference on the list established as a result of such test. Preference means that to the score of a veteran who has passed a test five points shall be added, and to the score of a disabled veteran who has passed a test ten points shall be added. All such points shall be added to the total combined test score of the veteran and shall not be allocated to any single feature or part of the examination. Rating shall be based on a scale of one hundred points as the maximum attainable except for the addition of the preference points allowed under this section.

### Section 408.235. Eligibility for preference; limitation on use

(1) Except for a veteran described in subsection (2) of this section, a veteran is eligible to use the preference provided for in ORS 408.230 only for a position for which application is made within fifteen years of discharge or release from service in the armed forces. Such time limit shall not apply in the case of a disabled veteran.

(2) A veteran whose service in the armed forces of the U.S. occurred between January 1, 1962 and May 7, 1975 within the borders of Vietnam, Cambodia, Laos or Thailand may use the preference provided for in ORS 408.230 only for a position for which application is made by July 1, 1999.

(3) Once a veteran has used the preference provided for in ORS 408.230 and has successfully completed trial service and attained regular employee status, the veteran may not use the preference again. Such limitation shall not apply in the case of a disabled veteran.

(4) Notwithstanding ORS 408.230 and subsections (1) to (3) of this section, a veteran whose service on active duty in the armed forces of the U.S. occurred entirely on or after October 15, 1976, may not use the preference provided for in ORS 408.230 unless the veteran was in the theater of operations when the armed forces of the U.S. were engaged in armed conflict with military forces of another nation or with terrorist or other armed forces.

# PENNSYLVANIA
### (Pennsylvania Consolidated Statutes)

### Chapter 71, Section 7101. Soldier defined

As used in this chapter, "soldier" means a person who served in the armed forces of the United States, or in any women's organization officially connected therewith, during any war or armed conflict in which the U.S. engaged, or who so served or hereafter serves in the armed forces of the U.S., or in any women's organization officially connected therewith, since July 27, 1953, including service in Vietnam, and who has an honorable discharge from such service.

### Section 7102. Credits in civil service examinations

(a) General rule—When any soldier shall take any civil service appointment or promotional examination for a public position under the Commonwealth, or any political subdivision thereof, he shall be given credit in the manner hereinafter provided; for the discipline and experience represented by his military training and for the loyalty and public spirit demonstrated by his service for the preservation of his country, as provided in this chapter.

(b) Disclosure of rank or serial number—No soldier taking any civil service appointment or promotional examination shall be required to furnish, nor shall he furnish in connection therewith, his former rank or service serial number.

### Section 7103. Additional points in grading civil service examinations

(a) Commonwealth examinations—Whenever any soldier shall successfully pass a civil service appointment or promotional examination for a public position under this Commonwealth, or any political subdivision thereof, and shall thus establish that he possesses the qualifications required by law for appointment to or promotion in such public position, such soldier's examination shall be marked or graded an additional ten points above the mark or grade credited for the examination, and the total mark or grade thus obtained shall represent the final mark or grade of such soldier, and shall determine his standing on any eligible or promotional list, certified or furnished to the appointing or promoting power

(b) Municipal examinations—When any such person shall take any examination for appointment or promotion in the civil service of any of the various municipal agencies within this Commonwealth, as required by any existing law or any law which may hereafter be enacted, such person's examination shall be marked or graded 15% perfect before the quality or contents of the examination shall be considered. When the examination of any such person is completed and graded, such grading or percentage as the examination merits shall be added to the aforesaid 15%, and such total mark or grade shall represent the final grade or classification of such person and shall determine his or her order of standing on the eligible list.

### Section 39405. Grading for discharged servicemen

When any person who was engaged in the military service of the U.S. during any military engagement in which the U.S. participated, and has an honorable discharge therefrom, shall take any examination for appointment or promotion, his examination shall be marked or graded in the same manner as provided for in all other examinations. When the examination of any such person is completed and graded, if the grade is passing, then such grading or percentage as the examination merits shall be increased by fifteen percentum, and such total mark or grade shall represent the final grade or classification of such person and shall determine his or her order of standing on the eligible list. For the purpose of this article, the military service means the army, navy, marines, air force, coast guard and any branch or unit thereof; and servicemen means the members thereof, including women; and military engagement includes land, naval and air engagements.

# RHODE ISLAND
## (General Laws of Rhode Island)

### Section 30-21-8. Preference in public employment; Notice to community service division

In every public department and upon all public works of this state, any honorably discharged soldier, sailor or marine who served in the army or navy of the United States during the Spanish-American War, Philippine Insurrection, China Relief Expedition, or World War I, and who, having been disabled in service, and at the time of his or her application for employment, is a qualified elector of this state, shall be preferred for appointment and employment. Age, loss of limb or other physical impairment which does not in fact incapacitate, shall not disqualify the veteran, if he or she possesses the other requisite qualifications. Whenever any department, division, bureau, board or commission in this state shall have a vacant position available, the department, division, bureau, board or commission shall notify the assistant director of human services in charge of the community services division that a vacancy exists.

### Section 30-21-12. Appointment to police or fire forces

Any citizen who has served in the military service of the United States, in the army, navy or air force thereof, and who has received an honorable discharge therefrom, may be eligible for appointment as a police officer or firefighter in any city or town of this state in the same manner as though that citizen were a qualified elector of the city or town on the date of his or her appointment; provided, however, that the citizen, if registered at any time during the military service, would be a qualified elector of that city or town at the date of that appointment.

### Section 30-21-13. Extension of credits, benefits and privileges

All credits, benefits and privileges excepting bonuses, granted and bestowed as of December 7, 1941 by this state upon men and women in the armed forces, shall be extended to include those veterans of the Desert Storm Conflict beginning August 2, 1990 and continuing to the present, honorably discharged from active duty.

### Section 30-22-1. World War II veterans

The provisions of all of the statutes of this state granting benefits or privileges to veterans of any war in which the United States has heretofore been engaged, or to the widow or widower or other surviving kin of deceased veterans of that war, shall hereafter be construed to provide for like benefits and privileges for any veteran of World War II and who has heretofore or may hereafter be honorably discharged from the armed forces, and to the widow or widower or other surviving kin of deceased veterans of that war.

### Section 30-22-2. Merchant Marine

(a) All credits, benefits and privileges, excepting bonuses, granted and bestowed as of December 7, 1941 by this state upon men and women in the armed forces of the U.S. and then enjoyed by those armed forces, shall be extended to include members of the American Merchant Marine Service who, at the date of enlistment, were legal residents of this state; provided, however, that those members of the American Merchant Marine shall have been in service for at least six months, but in the event any member shall meet death before the expiration of that six months of service he or she shall receive all credits, benefits and privileges to which he or she would have been entitled by this section had death not inter-vened in that six months' service.

(b) All eligible members under this section shall file with the department of veterans affairs for a discharge certificate on forms provided by the department of veterans affairs for that purpose.

**Section 30-22-3.** Veterans of undeclared wars or campaigns

The provisions of all of the statutes of this state granting benefits or privileges to veterans of any war in which the United States has heretofore been engaged, or to the widow or widower or other surviving kin of deceased veterans of that war, shall hereafter be construed to provide for like benefits and privileges for any man or woman of the armed forces who has been engaged heretofore, is now, or may hereafter be engaged in the active conduct of and/or fighting in the Korean Campaign or the conflict in Vietnam or any following campaign or war, declared or undeclared, which the armed forces of the U.S. conduct or in which those forces have a part, and who, having been actively engaged as hereinbefore described, has heretofore or may hereafter be honorably discharged from the armed forces, and to the widow or widower or other surviving kin of any such deceased veteran of that campaign or war.

**Section 30-22-5.** "Vietnam Service" defined

"Active conduct of and/or fighting in the Vietnam Conflict" shall mean service by any man or woman of the armed forces of the U.S. between December 22, 1961 and May 7, 1975, inclusive. Provided, however, that the extension of the date from August 5, 1964 to December 22, 1961 in the definition of the Vietnam Conflict shall not entitle any veteran who served between December 22, 1961 and August 5, 1964 to any bonus previously paid.

# SOUTH CAROLINA
## (Code of Laws of South Carolina)

**Article 7, Section 1-1-550.** Honorably discharged veterans shall have preference for public employment

Honorably discharged members of the United States Armed Forces who are given employment preference by the U.S. Government, now and hereafter, shall be given preference for appointment and employment in every public department and upon all public works of this state insofar as such preference may be practicable; age, loss of limb or other physical impairment which does not in fact incapacitate shall not be deemed to disqualify them, provided they possess the capacity of skill and knowledge necessary to discharge the duties of the position involved. Provided, that any public department operating on a merit system shall give preferences similar to those given by the U.S. Government to eligible members discharged from the Armed Forces insofar as such preferences may be practicable.

# SOUTH DAKOTA
## (South Dakota Codified Laws)

**Section 3-3-1.** Veterans preferred in public employment; Age or physical impairment not to disqualify; Disabled veterans preferred over non-disabled

In all public departments and subdivisions and upon all public works of this state and of the counties and municipalities thereof, honorably discharged soldiers, sailors, marines and nurses of the Spanish-American War, Philippine Insurrection or China Relief Expedition, and veterans as that term is defined in section 33-17-1, who are citizens and residents of this state, shall be preferred for appointment, employment and promotion; age, loss of limb or other physical impairment which does not in fact incapacitate, shall not be deemed to disqualify them, provided they possess the qualifications and business capacity necessary to discharge the duties of the position involved. A veteran disabled due to a service-connected cause shall be given a preference over a non-disabled veteran.

**Section 33-17-1.** General definition of veteran

For the purposes of all statutes relating to rights, privileges, exemptions and benefits (except a state bonus) of veterans and their orphans and other dependents, the term "veteran" means any person who:

(1) has performed qualifying military service as defined in section 33-17-2; and

(2) has been separated or discharged from the armed forces honorably or under honorable conditions or has been released to any reserve component of the armed forces of the U.S.

**Section 33-17-2.** Periods of service qualifying for veterans' benefits

As used in section 33-17-1, the term "qualifying military service" means:

(1) Active duty in the armed forces of the U.S. for one day or more during the period from April 6, 1917 to November 11, 1918, inclusive;

(2) Active duty for one day or more during the period from July 28, 1914

to November 11, 1918, inclusive, performed by a citizen of the U.S. in the armed forces of any nation that was allied with the United States during any part of the period from April 6, 1917 to November 11, 1918, inclusive;

(3) Active duty in the armed forces of the U.S. for one day or more during the period from December 7, 1941 to December 31, 1946, inclusive;

(4) Active duty for one day or more during the period from September 1, 1939 to December 31, 1946, inclusive, performed by a citizen of the U.S. in the armed forces of any nation that was allied with the United States during any part of the period from December 7, 1941 to December 31, 1946, inclusive;

(5) Active duty in the armed forces of the U.S. for one day or more during the period from June 25, 1950 to May 7, 1975, inclusive;

(6) Active duty in the armed forces of the U.S. for one day or more during the period from August 2, 1990 to March 3, 1991, inclusive;

(7) Active duty in the armed forces of the U.S. for one day or more in a military action for which the veteran earned an armed forces expeditionary medal, southwest Asia service medal or other United States campaign or service medal awarded for participation outside the boundaries of the U.S. in combat operations against hostile forces; or

(8) Active duty in the armed forces of the U.S. for one day or more if the veteran has established the existence of a service-connected disability.

Any reserve or national guard personnel who have served on active duty for training shall not be construed thereby to have served on active duty, unless the veterans' commission determines, by rules promulgated pursuant to chapter 1-26 that such training involved the person in direct participation in or direct support of combat operations against a hostile force.

Section 33-17-2.1. Benefits extended to veterans serving since 1955

To the extent and for the purposes for which veterans of World War I, World War II or the Korean Conflict, their orphans or other dependents are or were entitled under existing law to certain rights, privileges, exemptions and benefits, these rights, exemptions, privileges and benefits, except a state bonus, are hereby extended to any person who has served on active duty with the armed forces of the U.S. between February 1, 1955 and April 1, 1973, who has been discharged from such service honorably or under honorable conditions, or has been released to any reserve branch of the armed forces of the U.S.; or any active duty personnel whose service has qualified them for such benefits. Any reserve or national guard personnel who have served on active duty for training may not be construed to have served on active duty.

*(South Dakota Personnel Regulations)*

### Section 55:01:05:10. Veterans' Preference

The Commissioner shall grant veterans' preference in accordance with SDCL 3-3-1 to any applicant who is otherwise eligible for state employment and who requests such preference on the application. To receive preference, the veteran must submit a copy of the discharge papers and, for disability credit, proof from the U.S. Veterans Administration that the disability is at least ten percent. All applicants shall first be rated on examinations and the top scorers selected. The applicants who are veterans shall then have five points added to their scores with an additional five points added for a service-connected disability. If the veteran's score, with preference, is equivalent to or higher than the lowest score on the certification, the applicant shall be added to the certification.

# TENNESSEE
*(Tennessee Code)*

### Section 8-30-306. Veterans' preference points

(1) Any person who has been honorably discharged from the army, navy, air force or marine corps, who served in the armed forces of the U.S. during the period of a war, the Korean Conflict, the Vietnam Conflict. The Lebanon Expedition, the Grenada Expedition, the Panama Expedition or Operation Desert Storm, shall have five points added to such person's earned rating in examination for entrance to the career service; provided, that such person is a qualified voter in this state or has been a resident of this state for two years next preceding such person's application; and provided further that for purposes of establishing preference points for the Lebanon Expedition, the Grenada Expedition or the Panama Expedition, points shall be awarded only to veterans who received the Armed Forces Expeditionary Medal.

(2) If such veteran is disabled as a result of such military service, such veteran shall have ten points added to such veteran's rating, if the com-

missioner determines that such disability will not impair such veteran's fitness for the position sought.

(3) The spouse or surviving spouse of any one hundred percent (100%) service-connected disabled veteran whose disability resulted from such military service shall have ten points added to such person's rating; provided, that such surviving spouse shall not have remarried since the death of such person's veteran spouse.

(4) The spouse or surviving spouse of any permanently disabled veteran whose disability resulted from military service, or veteran who died in the line of duty, during a period other than a period of war, the Korean Conflict, the Vietnam Conflict, the Lebanon Expedition, the Grenada Expedition, the Panama Expedition or Operation Desert Storm shall have five points added to such spouse or surviving spouse's rating; provided, that such surviving spouse shall have not remarried since the death of the veteran; provided further that, for the purposes of establishing preference points for the Lebanon Expedition, the Grenada Expedition or the Panama Expedition, points shall be awarded only to veterans who received the Armed Forces Expeditionary Medal.

(5) In entering upon registers the names of preference claimants entitled to additional points, they will take the place to which their ratings entitled them on the register with non-veterans, that is, the earned ratings augmented by the points to which they are entitled, and will be certified when their ratings are reached. The name of a veteran with the augmented rating will be entered ahead of the name of a non-veteran when their ratings are the same.

# TEXAS
## (Texas Code)

### Section 657.001. Definitions

In this chapter:

(1) "Established service-connected disability" means a disability that has been or may be established by official records.

(2) "Public entity" means a public department, commission, board or agency.

### Section 657.002. Individuals entitled to veteran's employment preference

(a) A veteran or the widow or orphan of a veteran qualifies for a veteran's employment preference if the veteran:

    (1) served in the military during:

        (A) the Spanish-American War;

        (B) the Philippine Insurrection;

        (C) the China Relief Expedition;

        (D) World War I;

        (E) World War II;

        (F) Any other military conflict in which the U.S. was a participant before June 18, 1945;

        (G) The Korean War after June 24, 1950; or

        (H) The Vietnam Conflict after July, 1953

    (2) was honorably discharged from military service; and

    (3) is competent.

(b) This chapter does not apply to a veteran who;

    (1) was a conscientious objector at the time of the veteran's discharge from military service; or

    (2) is receiving or entitled to receive military retirement pay, other than disability retirement pay, from the United States.

(c) In this section, "veteran" means an individual who served in the army, navy, marine corps, or coast guard of the United States or in an auxiliary service of one of those branches of the armed forces.

### Section 657.003. Veteran's employment preference

(a) An individual who qualifies for a veteran's employment preference is entitled to a preference in employment with or appointment to a public entity or for a public work of this state over other applicants for the same position who do not have a greater qualification.

(b) An individual who has an established service-connected disability and is entitled to a veteran's employment preference is entitled to preference for employment or appointment in a position for which a competitive examination is not held over all other applicants for the same position without a service-connected disability and who do not have a greater qualification.

(c) If a public entity or public work of this state requires a competitive examination under a merit system or civil service plan for selecting or promoting employees, an individual entitled to a veteran's employment preference who otherwise is qualified for that position and who has received at least the minimum required score for the test is entitled to have a service credit of ten points added to the test score. An individual who has an established service-connected disability is entitled to have a service credit of five additional points added to the individual's test score.

(d) An individual entitled to a veteran's employment preference is not disqualified from holding a position with a public entity or public work of this state because of age or an established service-connected disability if the age or disability does not make the individual incompetent to perform the duties of the position.

# UTAH
## (Utah Code)

### Section 71-10-1. Definitions

As used in this chapter:

(1) "Active duty" means active military duty and does not include active duty for training, initial active duty for training, or inactive duty for training.

(2) "Disabled veteran" means an individual who has:

(a) been separated or retired from the armed forces under honorable conditions; and

(b) established the existence of a service-connected disability or is receiving compensation, disability retirement benefits or a pension because of a public statute administered by the federal Department of Veterans Affairs or a military department.

(3) "Government entity" means the state and any county, municipality, special district or any other political subdivision or administrative unit of the state.

(4) "Preference eligible" means:

(a) any individual who has served on active duty in the armed forces for more than one hundred eighty consecutive days, or was a member of a reserve component who served in a campaign or expedition for which a campaign medal has been authorized and who has been separated under honorable conditions;

(b) a disabled veteran with any percentage of disability;

(c) the unmarried widow or widower of a veteran;

(d) a Purple Heart recipient; or

(e) a retired member of the armed forces who retired below the rank of major or its equivalent.

(5) "Veteran" means:

(a) an individual who has served on active duty in the armed forces for more than 180 consecutive days, or was a member of a reserve component who served in a campaign or expedition for which a campaign medal has been authorized and who has been separated under honorable conditions;

(b) any person incurring an actual service-related injury or disability whether or not that person completed 180 days of active duty.

## Section 71-10-2. Veteran's preference

(1) Each government entity shall grant a veteran's preference upon initial hiring to each preference eligible veteran or preference eligible spouse according to the procedures and requirements of this chapter.

(2) The personnel officer of any government entity shall add to the score of a preference eligible who receives a passing score on an examination, or any rating or ranking mechanism used in selecting an individual for any career service position with that government entity;

(a) five percent of the total possible score, if he is a veteran;

(b) ten percent of the total possible score, if he is a disabled veteran or a Purple Heart recipient; or

(c) in the case of a preference eligible widow or widower, the same percentage the qualifying veteran would have been entitled to.

(3) A preference eligible who applies for a position that does not require an examination, or where examination results are other than a numeric score, shall be given preference in interviewing and hiring for the position.

# VERMONT
## (Vermont Statutes)

**Chapter 83, Section 1543.** Preferences for appointment to state positions

In certification for appointment, in appointment, in employing, in retention of employment positions, whether in classified or unclassified civil service, whether for temporary or for an extended time, wherever state funds furnish the payroll, preference shall be given to:

(1) those ex-service personnel who have served on active duty in any branch of the armed forces of the U.S. and have been separated therefrom under honorable conditions and who have established the present existence of a service-connected disability or who are receiving compensation or disability retirement benefits by reason of public laws administered by the Veterans Administration, or the Department of Defense;

(2) the spouses of such service-connected disabled ex-servicemen or women as have themselves been unable to qualify for any civil service appointment by reason of their disability;

(3) the unmarried widow or widowers of deceased ex-service personnel who served on active duty in any branch of the armed forces of the U.S. during any war, or in any campaign or expedition for which a campaign badge has been authorized, or during the periods specified in subdivision (5) of this section and who were separated therefrom under honorable conditions; and

(4) those ex-service personnel who served on active duty in any branch of the armed forces of the U.S. during any war, or in any campaign or expedition for which a campaign badge has been authorized, and who have been separated therefrom under honorable conditions; and

(5) those ex-service personnel who served on active duty in any branch of the armed forces of the U.S. during the period beginning July 1, 1955 and have been separated from the armed forces under honorable conditions.

## Title 3, Section 310. Classification plan; rules

The classification and compensation plan and the rules and regulations for personnel administration shall be based on merit system principles and shall provide for compliance with the laws relating to preference granted to qualified persons who have served in the armed forces of the U.S. and received an honorable discharge, so that veterans who meet the requirements for any open competitive examination and who receive a passing score shall have five points added to their competitive examination rating; and service-connected disabled veterans, veterans' widows or widowers, and spouses of totally service-connected disabled veterans who meet the requirements for any open competitive examination and who receive a passing score shall have ten points added to their competitive examination rating, subject to the provisions contained in Section 1543 of Title 20. Except when the monthly service retirement allowance of any individual at the time of application was more than the median of all different armed forces monthly net allowances existing at the time of application, then there shall be no veteran's preference given.

# VIRGINIA
## (Code of Virginia)

**Section 2.1-112.** Grade or rating increase and other preferences for veterans

A. In the event a person who has served in the armed forces of the United States in World War I, World War II, the Korean War or the Vietnam War, having an honorable discharge, is an applicant for a position in the state service which is filled after an examination given by the Merit System Council under the merit system plan applicable to personnel employed by the Virginia Employment Commission, the state and local boards of public welfare, the State Board of Health, and the Virginia Department For The Visually Handicapped, or any other state agency whose employees are so examined, the grade or rating of the applicant on such examination shall be increased by five percent. If such applicant shall have a service-connected disability rating fixed by the U.S. Veterans Administration, his grade shall be increased by ten percent. Such additions shall only be made if any such applicant passes such examination.

B. In the event that any person mentioned in subsection (A) applies for employment with any agency of the Commonwealth where examinations are not required of the applicants, such person shall be assured that his service with the armed forces shall be taken into consideration by the agency during the selection process, provided that such person meets all of the knowledge, skill and ability requirements for the vacancy. Each agency of the Commonwealth shall take affirmative action consistent with its obligations for protected classes.

# WASHINGTON
## (Revised Code of Washington)

**Section 41.04.004.** "Veteran" defined

As used in RCW 41.04.005, 41.04.010, 41.16.220 and 41.20.050, "veteran" includes every person who, at the time he seeks the benefits of RCW 28B.40.361, 41.01.005, 41.04.010, 41.16.220, 41.20.050, 41.40.170, 73.04.110 or 73.08.080, has received an honorable discharge or received a discharge for physical reasons with an honorable record and: (1) has served in any branch of the armed forces of the United States between World War I and World War II or during any period of war; or (2) has served in any branch of the armed forces of the U.S. and has received the armed forces expeditionary medal, or the Marine Corps and Navy Expeditionary Medal, for opposed action on foreign soil. A "period of war" includes World War I, World War II, the Korean Conflict, the Vietnam Conflict and the period beginning on the date of any future declaration of war by the Congress and ending on the date prescribed by Presidential Proclamation or concurrent resolution of the Congress. The "Vietnam Era" means the period beginning August 5, 1964 and ending on May 7, 1975.

**Section 41.04.010.** Veterans' preference in examinations

In all competitive examinations, unless otherwise provided herein, to determine the qualifications of applicants for public offices, positions or employment, the state and all of its political subdivisions and all municipal corporations shall give a preference status to all veterans as defined in RCW 41.04.005, by adding to the passing mark, grade or rating only, based upon a possible rating of one hundred points as a perfect percentage, in accordance with the following:

(1) ten percent to a veteran who is not receiving any veterans retirement payments and said percentage shall be utilized in said veteran's competitive examination and not in any promotional examination until one of such examinations results in said veteran's first appointment: **Provided,** that said percentage shall not be utilized in any promotional examination;

(2) five percent to a veteran who is receiving any veterans retirement payments and said percentage shall be utilized in said veteran's competitive examination only and not in any promotional examination until one of such examinations results in said veteran's first appointment; **Provided,** that said percentage shall not be utilized in any promotional examination;

(3) five percent to a veteran who, after having previously received employment with the state or any of its political subdivisions or municipal corporations, shall be called, or recalled to active military service for a period of one year or more, during any period of war, for his first promotional examination only, upon compliance with RCW 73.16.035 as it now exists or may hereafter be amended;

(4) There shall be no examination preferences other than those which have been specifically provided for above and all preferences above specified in (1), (2) and (3) must be claimed by a veteran within eight years of the date of his release from active service.

Section 73.04.090. Benefits, preferences, exemptions, etc.; limited to veterans subject to full, continuous military control

All benefits, advantages or emoluments, not available upon equal terms to all citizens, including but not limited to preferred rights to public employment, civil service preference, exemption from license fees or other impositions, preference in purchasing state property and special pension or retirement rights, which by any law of this state have been made specially available to war veterans or to persons who have served in the armed forces or defense forces of the United States, shall be available only to persons who have been subject to full and continuous military control and discipline as actual members of the federal armed forces. Service with such forces in a civilian capacity or in any capacity wherein a person retained the right to terminate his service or to refuse full obedience to military superiors, shall not be the basis for eligibility for such benefits. Service in any of the following shall not for the purposes of this section be considered military service: The Office of Emergency Services or any component thereof; the American Red Cross; the U.S. Coast Guard Auxiliary; United States Coast Guard Reserve Temporary; the U.S. Coast & Geodetic Survey; the American Field Service; the Civil Air Patrol; the Cadet Nurse Corps and any other similar organization.


# WEST VIRGINIA
## (West Virginia Code)


Section 6-13-1. Preference rating for veterans on written examinations for positions in state departments filled under nonpartisan merit system

For positions in any department or agency in which positions are filled under civil service or any job classification system, a preference of five points in addition to the regular numerical score received on an examination shall be awarded to all veterans having qualified for appointment by making a minimum passing grade; and to all veterans awarded the Purple Heart or having a compensable service-connected disability, as established by any proper veteran's bureau or department of the federal government, an additional five points shall be allowed.

For the purpose of this article, "veteran" shall mean any person who has served in the armed forces of the United States during the Spanish-American War, World War I, World War II, the Korean Conflict, the Southeast Asian Conflict or in a campaign, expedition or conflict for which a campaign badge has been authorized and received by such person, and who has been honorably discharged from such service.

Such awards shall be made for the benefit and preference in appointment for all veterans who have heretofore or who shall hereafter take such examinations, but shall not operate to the detriment of any person heretofore appointed to a position in such department or agency.

# WISCONSIN
## (Wisconsin Statutes)

### Section 230.16. Applications and examinations
### Section 230.16(1)(a)

Competitive examinations shall be free and open to all applicants who at the time of application are residents of this state and who have fulfilled the preliminary requirements stated in the examination announcement. To assure that all residents of this state have a fair opportunity to compete, examinations shall be held at such times and places as, in the judgment of the administrator, most nearly meet the convenience of applicants and the needs of the service. If a critical need for employees in specific classifications or positions exists, then the administrator may open competitive examinations to persons who are not residents of this state.

### Section 230.16(b)(7)

A preference shall be given to any qualifying veteran who gains eligibility on any competitive employment register and who does not currently hold a permanent appointment or have mandatory restoration rights to a permanent appointment to any position. A preference means that if a veteran gains eligibility on any employment register and does not currently hold a permanent appointment or have mandatory restoration rights to a permanent appointment to any position, five points shall be added to his or her grade. If a veteran has a disability which is directly traceable to war service, the veteran shall be accorded a total of ten points. "Veteran" as used in this subsection means any person who served on active duty under honorable conditions in the armed forces of the U.S. and who was entitled to receive either the armed forces expeditionary medal, established by executive order 10977 on 4 December 1961, or the Vietnam Service Medal established by executive order 11231 on 8 July 1965, or who served in Grenada or Lebanon under s. 45.34 or any person who served for at least one day during a war period, as defined in s. 45.35(5)(a) to (g) or under section one of executive order 10957 dated 10 August 1961.

*Section 45.35(5)(a).* Veteran defined

"Veteran" as used in this chapter, except in s. 45.37 and unless otherwise modified, means any person who has served on active duty under honorable conditions in the armed forces of the U.S. or in forces incorporated as part of the U.S. armed forces, except service on active duty for training purposes, and who meets the following conditions:

(1) The person is a resident of and living in this state at the time of making application, or is deceased, and meets one of the following conditions:

(a) has served in Bosnia, Grenada, Lebanon, Panama, Somalia or in a Middle East crisis under s. 45.34;

(b) was entitled to receive the armed forces expeditionary medal, established by executive order 10977 on 4 December 1961, the Vietnam Service Medal established by executive order 11231 on 8 July 1965, the Navy Expeditionary Medal or the Marine Corps Expeditionary Medal;

(c) has served for ninety days or more during a war period as enumerated under par. (e) or under section one of executive order 10957 dated 10 August 1961, or if having served less than ninety days was honorably discharged for a service-connected disability or for a disability subsequently adjudicated to have been service-connected or died in the service.

(2) The person is a resident of and living in this state at the time of making application or is deceased, and meets one of the following conditions:

(a) his or her selective service board, if any, and home of record at the time of entry or reentry into active service as shown on the veteran's report of separation from the armed forces of the U.S. for a qualifying period were in this state;

(b) was a resident of this state at the time of entry or reentry into active duty;

(c) has been a resident of this state for any consecutive five-year period after completing service on active duty and before his or her application or death. If a person applying for a benefit under this subchapter meets that five consecutive year residency requirement, the department may not require the person to reestablish that he or she meets the five consecutive year residency requirement when he or she later applies for any other benefit under this chapter that requires a five consecutive year residency.

### Section 45.35(5)(b)

If the person had more than one qualifying term of service under par. (a)(1), at least one term of service must have been under honorable conditions or have been terminated by an honorable discharge for the purpose of establishing eligibility under this section and s. 45.37(1a).

### Section 45.35(5)(c)

Veterans who are otherwise eligible and who are serving on active duty in the U.S. armed forces need not be living in this state on the date of application to qualify for benefits from the department.

### Section 45.35(5)(d)

The benefits available to veterans are also available to the unremarried surviving spouses and minor or dependent children of deceased veterans if the unremarried surviving spouses or minor or dependent children are residents of and living in this state at the time of making application.

### Section 45.35(5m). Dependent defined

(a) "Dependent" of a veteran as used in this section and section 45.351 includes only:

(1) a wife or husband, an unremarried widow or widower; or a divorced wife only when receiving benefits under a court order.

(2) Any child of the veteran under eighteen years of age, or under the age of twenty-six if in full attendance at a recognized school of instruction, or of any age if incapable of self-support by reason of mental or

physical disability. "Child" as used in this section means any natural child, any legally adopted child, any stepchild or child if a member of the veteran's household or any nonmarital child if the veteran acknowledges paternity or the same has been otherwise established.

(b) For purposes of defining "dependent" under this subsection, "veteran" includes a person who served on active duty under honorable conditions in the U.S. armed forces, who was a resident of this state at the time of entry or reentry into active duty and who died while on active duty if that death was not the result of the veteran's willful misconduct.

(c) The natural mother or natural father or a person to whom the veteran stands in the place of a parent and who has so stood for not less than twelve months prior to the veteran's entrance into active service.

(d) A minor sister or minor brother or a brother or sister of any age if incapable of self-support by reason of mental or physical disability.

# WYOMING
## (Wyoming Statutes)

**Section 19-6-102.** Employment; preference in public departments or public works; qualifications and residence

(a) In every public department and upon all public works in this state, members of the U.S. military establishment in any war or conflict as defined in 38 U. S. C. 101, honorably discharged from the service, and the widows of members during widowhood, shall be preferred for appointment or employment. Age or other physical impairment which does not in fact incapacitate shall not disqualify them from receiving preference if they possess the business capacity, competency, education or other qualifications for discharge of the duties required. If the disabilities do not materially interfere with performance of the duties, the disabled veterans or widows shall be given preference over employment of able-bodied veterans and widows. A veteran or widow who has not been a resident of this state for a period of one year or more immediately preceding the date for appointment or employment is not entitled to preference under this section and for municipal or county employment, no preference shall be granted unless the applicant under this section is a resident of the municipality or county in which employment is sought.

(b) Each official or person having power of appointment in the public service is charged with the faithful compliance with the duties herein prescribed.

(c) Whenever a veteran of any war or conflict as defined in 38 U. S. C. 101 takes any examination under the merit system of this state, the veteran shall be allowed a five (5) point advantage over any non-veteran competitor for the same position or proposed employment, and if the veteran has a service-connected disability of ten percent (10%) or more, the advantage given shall be ten (10) points. This section applies only to *bona fide* residents of Wyoming at the time of their entry into the armed service of the U.S. and who are at the time of taking the examination *bona fide* residents of Wyoming.

# SPECIAL MENTION:
# STATES WITH APPRECIATIVE
# OR NOTABLY BENEFICIAL
# STATUTES

The state statutes listed below bear special mention because certain attributes are either unique or peculiar to a few states. The following section is divided into (1) those states which expressly convey in the language of the law their appreciation to veterans for their military service, and (2) those states which the author regards as the most appreciative in terms of the benefits which are bestowed by law.

## APPRECIATION CONVEYED BY LAW

It could go without saying that the general purpose of all the statutes in this book is to convey to honorably discharged veterans the appreciation of state governments. Every state legislature has sought to express through legislated benefits their gratitude for the sacrifices which veterans have made and continue to make for this republic. This is the reason why every governmental entity listed herein requires that veterans be hired before others who did not serve.

The appreciation that state governments convey sometimes goes beyond the preference points which are added to the score which a veteran achieves on a civil service examination. The statutes of a few states explicitly declare their admiration for the veteran's tenure in uniform. For this reason they deserve special mention in this book. These states and their respective statutes where such language is found are:

(1) Kansas, section 73-201
(2) Minnesota, section 43A.11
(3) North Carolina, section 126-80
(4) Pennsylvania, Chap. 51, section 7102(a)

# THE MOST VETERAN-FRIENDLY STATES

This book attempts to convey the vast array of statutes which favor veterans and also their varying nature. A review of the information in this book clearly reveals that some states are more generous to veterans than are others. The states which the author regards as the most "veteran-friendly" are cited below. The reader is further referred to the Quick Reference Guide, which facilitates examination of the laws discussed below.

## HAWAII

Hawaii (HI) deserves special mention because unlike most states, it requires only that one be a veteran, i.e., not a veteran of a war or a campaign, in order to receive employment preference (five points). As is typical of the states, HI awards disabled veterans five additional points, or ten total. Hawaii also awards Purple Heart recipients the same number of points as disabled veterans (ten points).

Other peculiarities in the HI statute include the fact that HI grants preference to persons who did not serve in the U.S. Armed Forces but in forces which were allied to the U.S. during hostilities. The only qualifier here is that the veteran of another nation's armed force be a U.S. citizen when applying for the preference.

Coupling the above facts with the fact that HI grants retirees the same amount of preference as that which is given to regular veterans makes HI quite veteran friendly and therefore deserving of special recognition.

## WISCONSIN

Like HI, Wisconsin (WI) stipulates that retirees receive the same preference as regular veterans (five points). In addition, WI deserves special mention because it is one of the few states which stipulates that veterans who were subjected to the Selective Service Act (conscription) are entitled to employment preference. One need not have been a veteran of a war or hostilities in order to receive employment preference.

What is most prominent about the WI statute, however, is that WI is the only state which apparently allows persons who have not yet been discharged from the service to apply for state employment and therefore employment preference. The pertinent part of the statute is Section 45.35(5)(c). This benefit is all the more significant in view of the fact that WI requires that one be a resident, though not actually residing within the state, in order to apply for employment preference.

Accordingly, the WI statute allows a person who is about to leave the service to be examined for employment and also to apply for the preference prior to discharge. Vets can thus take necessary steps to secure state employment in anticipation of discharge and possibly have a job waiting upon release from active duty. WI is therefore quite veteran-friendly.

## OKLAHOMA

Oklahoma (OK) provides for special permits and tax exemptions in addition to the regular employment preference. This can be observed in Chap. 72, section 67.13a. OK is further unique in the fact that it is the only state in the Union where veteran employees are given credit for military service when computing retirement benefits in the state service. This provision also applies to military retirees. Also significant is the fact that the law does not stipulate that one's job in the military must have been related to one's position in the state civil service.

OK further stipulates that (1) a person only be a veteran, i.e., not a war veteran, in order to claim employment preference; (2) retirees receive the same preference as regular veterans; (3) preference must be given to all veterans who were subjected to the Selective Service Act; and (4) disabled veterans be placed at the top of a register. These facts, together with the statutes previously mentioned, make OK one of the most veteran-friendly states in the Union.

## OHIO

Ohio (OH) is deserving of special mention primarily because of the manner in which preference is given to veterans. The OH law requires that any passing score which a qualifying veteran achieves on an examination is automatically augmented by 20 percent. This means that if a qualifying veteran achieves a score of 90 on an examination, then the final augmented score will rise to 108. This attribute makes OH the most veteran-friendly state in the Union, numerically speaking.

In addition, OH explicitly states that Coast Guard veterans must be included in its definition of "armed forces." Recall that some states fail to refer specifically to the Coast Guard in their statutes (although Coast Guard service may actually be qualifying in those states; refer to the chapter entitled "Overview of Federal and State Statutes," under Veteran defined/Veteran defined by branch of service). Recall also that some states explicitly exclude the Coast Guard from their definition of "armed forces." By explicitly including the Coast Guard in its definition, OH's veteran-friendly reputation is commensurately enhanced.

On the subject of inclusion of certain "types" of veterans, OH is deserving of special mention because it is one of the few states which provide that persons who were subjected to the Selective Service (conscription) laws of the U.S. are deserving of employment preference.

Further, as is shown on the Quick Reference Guide, OH requires that the state law which requires veterans to be preferred for employment also extends to counties and cities. It is not clear, however, if the law requires that preference in county or city service be numerically identical to that which the state confers.

Lastly, the fact that OH requires that retirees receive identical preference to that which non-retirees receive, in addition to the attributes which are listed above, makes OH one of the most veteran-friendly states.


PENNSYLVANIA

Pennsylvania (PA) is one of the most veteran-friendly of all of the states, even surpassing (in the opinion of this author) all of those states discussed above. The reason is that PA seems to have gone the extra mile to convey to veterans both appreciation for their service and solid benefits to help them become gainfully employed.

PA is one of the few states giving honorably discharged veterans a ten-point preference on an examination. What is most interesting and unique about PA, however, is that this state affords an added credit for applicants for employment with county and city governments. PA goes beyond merely requiring local governments to grant veterans credit on an examination, as do many states. PA requires that veteran applicants for employment with local governments be granted a 15 percent credit.

What is doubly unique about the PA statute is that it departs from the general wording of all of the other states in the manner in which it grants the credit with local governments. Recall that these types of statutes usually follow a standard pattern, requiring that a veteran first pass an examination before any veteran's preference credit can be added. (See

"Examinations" in the chapter entitled "Overview of Federal and State Statutes.") The PA statute requires that a veteran's examination be "marked or graded 15 percent perfect before the quality or contents of the examination shall be considered." This means that any honorably discharged veteran automatically starts with fifteen points on an examination.

Other highlights of the PA statute are that (1) the state formally recognizes the equality of the Coast Guard with the other four service branches (which some states do not); (2) retirees receive the same preference as regular veterans on examinations; and (3) preference is granted in both competitive and promotional examinations. This is not the case with most states. (See "One-Time Preference" in the chapter entitled "Overview of Federal and State Statutes.")

All of the above factors combine to make PA one of the top veteran-friendly states.

## MASSACHUSETTS

Refer to the Quick Reference Guide and examine the attributes for Massachusetts (MA). One should observe that there is no amount of veteran's credit indicated, as is the case with most of the states. The reason is that no numerical credit is applicable. MA is the only state which requires that veterans be hired before all others, irrespective of the score which the veteran attained on an examination. It is therefore immaterial for the statute to specify a numerical amount of preference.

The above fact alone makes MA the most veteran-friendly state. In addition, the fact that MA also (1) requires that preference apply to local governments, (2) requires that preference apply to public works projects, and (3) exempts recipients of special military decorations from having to be examined for employment, further enhances this state's status. Accordingly, MA appears to be the "Promised Land" for the honorably discharged veteran job seeker.

# THE QUICK REFERENCE GUIDE

This guide offers ready reference to the employment preference statutes of all fifty states, the District of Columbia, and the federal government. Using this guide, it is a simple matter to examine the basic attributes of these statutes, state by state—or to get a quick overall picture of a particular state's approach to employment preferences.

To find information concerning an individual state, look for the state in the alphabetical listing down the page. One should then read across the page to find the attributes which are listed for that state. Each attribute which pertains to the state in question is marked with an "X" or with a notation.

Alternatively, one may prefer to examine a particular attribute which is common to the laws of the several states or of the federal government. One should then look along the top of the guide and find the attribute that is of interest, then read down the page to find which states include that attribute in their laws.

Not all attributes pertain to every state. A blank box indicates that the state's laws do not include any language specific to that attribute. In some cases this lack of specific language may mean that certain restrictions do not apply to these states. For instance, with respect to attribute 7, "State Resident," most states have no language indicating that residency is required. This means that these states have no residency requirement as a prerequisite for claiming employment preference. Again, if one should require more precise details concerning a particular state, it is best to examine the applicable statute.

The numerical amount of preference which the laws require to be added to the passing scores of veterans' examinations is indicated in parentheses just beside the abbreviation for each state. State designations are those used by the U.S. Postal Service, but they are alphabetized as though spelled out. Federal law is represented by the abbreviation "U.S.," placed for convenience at the *end* of the list of states.

Note that two states, RI and FL, declined to specify a numerical preference in either the statute or the related personnel regulation. In two other states, MA and NJ, numerical preference is not applicable because of the peculiar language of those states' laws. Also, refer to the chapter entitled "State Statutes," which details the text of each state's law. Other than FL and RI, note that in each instance where the state declined to specify the amount of numerical preference in the statute, the attendant personnel regulation is included and will provide that information.

# ABOUT THE ATTRIBUTES IN THIS GUIDE

From state to state to the federal government, the laws pertaining to employment preferences for veterans share many attributes or characteristics. These attributes are common threads linking this series of laws together. They facilitate the analysis and comparison of the laws of differing jurisdictions.

The attributes most common among these laws are readily apparent when one examines any of the statutes. For purposes of this guide, the author has gleaned the most common attributes and organized them for quick reference.

The guide covers 53 attributes, of which there are two types: those common to most statutes, and those fairly unique to one or a few of the states and the federal government. Attributes of the first type demonstrate the common threads linking the statutes and facilitating their comparison. Attributes of the second type emphasize the manner in which the laws can vary among the governments.

For expediency the 53 attributes in the Guide (the charts) are in some cases abbreviated. These attributes require the following explanations:

## (1) Veteran

The term "veteran" as used here means that the states in question only require that the individual had served honorably in the military. The laws of these states decline to specify the dates during which the person must have served. Neither do these laws specify that the individual must have participated in a military campaign. In this regard, the only generic requirement which is usually specified is that one's duration of service must have been greater than 180 days, or that one must have served for activities other than for training. Note that each state which has this attribute marked also has attribute (47) similarly marked, but not vice-versa.

## (2) WAR VETERAN

These states have requirements which are in addition to those in category (1) above. In these states the veteran must have served during designated periods when this nation was engaged in hostilities with a foreign power. The precise dates are always specified within the text of the law. A reasonable assumption would therefore be that, conversely, those who did not serve during the dates indicated would be denied employment preference based on prior military service.

One should realize however that the law is dynamic. Laws change slowly but they do change, depending on the global military posture of the United States. It is possible for an individual to have served in the military during an interval which is not specified in the law, and still receive employment preference, if the individual served in specified military campaign. Even though the law may not explicitly specify the campaign, state legislatures are usually prompt in modifying the applicable statute to include military campaigns in which this nation has been involved. In these circumstances, if one requires the most recent update of the applicable state regulation, then one should contact the personnel officer of the state in question. There is more on this subject below.

## (3) VETERAN ONLY THROUGH VIETNAM

This attribute is an extension of (2) above. It deserves a special category in order to emphasize that some states have written their statutes only to include service up to the end of the Vietnam Conflict, which officially terminated on 7 May 1975. For the most part, this provision precludes veterans who served after the dates in question from receiving employment preference. However, to reiterate, this is not necessarily the case. The states and the federal government generally recognize their duty to modify statutes to include military campaigns in which the U.S. became engaged subsequent to the effective date of the statute in question.

The practice of state legislatures and of the U.S. Government to modify laws in this regard is further testimony to the appreciation which this nation shows to its military veterans. In examining the statutes which are included later in this book, one can observe that some states have modified their laws to include service in the Persian Gulf War of 1990-91, for example.

One should further observe that some states have written their statutes to include service in conflicts in which this nation may subsequently become involved.

## (4) ALL VETS MOVE TO TOP OF CERTIFICATE

The fact that the state in question, Massachusetts, prescribes this benefit is further testimony to this nation's appreciation for the sacrifices which veterans have made. The law requires that all veterans be placed at the top of the register or certificate which determines who will be hired first. As the author reads the statute, this benefit is prescribed for veterans irrespective of the individual's earned passing score on an examination. The law further requires that the benefit be given regardless of the interval during which the individual served in the military. Note that the state only requires that the individual be an honorably discharged veteran in order to be eligible for the preference.

## (5) ALL WAR VETS MOVE TO TOP OF CERTIFICATE

This attribute is an extension of (4) above. The only difference between this statute and the comparable law in Massachusetts is that one must be a war veteran. That is, one must have served during a specified period of hostilities. The law here requires that all such veterans be placed at the top of the certificate or register which determines who will be hired first. Again, the provision is in effect irrespective of the veteran's earned passing score on an examination.

## (6) CAMPAIGN BADGE NEEDED FOR PREFERENCE

One must either have received a badge or medal for having participated in a specified military campaign in order to be eligible for any preference, OR have served during a specified period of hostilities. Refer to (2) above. These two attributes always go together in this book. If an "X" is indicated for a state in category (2), then this attribute is also marked. One should remember however that it is always "either/or" when determining eligibility for the preference.

One should observe that if an individual participated in a military campaign and was therefore authorized to wear a badge or medal for having participated in such campaign, then one must by definition be a war veteran. Attribute (2) must therefore also apply. However, the reverse is not necessarily true.

## (7) State Residency

These states have residency requirements as a prerequisite to receiving employment preference. States that have residency requirements but do not specify a period of residency are marked with an "X." If a state specifies a required period of residency, that time period is indicated in lieu of the "X." The notation "Sp. Pro." means that the state in question has written special provisions into the law. In any case, one should examine the law carefully in order to determine the exact provisions. Some states simply prefer to hire state residents.

## (8) Residency Required (at Time of Application)

These states require that a veteran who applies for the preference be a resident of the state at the time that she or he applies. Where an "X" is indicated, the state does not specify an amount of time that one must have been a resident prior to applying for employment. Where a number of years are indicated, then this is the interval for which one must have been a resident of the state in order to be able to claim the preference. Note that the interval specified may not necessarily be the same amount of time that one must have been a resident in order to secure employment. Note also that the residency requirement is applicable only if one claims the preference. An individual has the option to decline the preference. Further, one may not have to verify residency in order to secure employment with the state. In other words, one may be able to decline the preference and still secure state employment. Provisions which govern these matters would be detailed in the state personnel regulations.

## (9) Prior Residency Required (at Time of Induction)

The states in question require that a veteran claiming the preference must have been a resident of the state at the time that he or she was inducted into the military. The procedure for verifying such residency would be detailed in the state personnel regulations.

## (10) Time Limit on Benefits After Discharge

The designated states have set a time limit on the amount of time during which a veteran can enjoy the benefit of employment preference. Presumably, the interval specified is that in which one can apply for and receive the preference. The time begins to run on the date that the veteran is discharged.

## (11) Time Limit to Apply for Preference

The law in this state provides that an individual has only a certain amount of time to apply for employment preference. Presumably the time begins to run on the date that the veteran is discharged.

## (12) Coast Guard Service Included

These states explicitly provide that service in the Coast Guard is qualifying to receive employment preference. Refer to the chapter "Overview of Federal and State Statutes," subhead "Veteran Defined by Branch of Service." Any potential debate on this subject is thereby eliminated by this provision.

## (13) Preference Extended to Spouse of Disabled

The spouse of a disabled veteran is eligible to receive employment preference. The number indicates the amount of the preference. An "*" indicates that the law for this state is such that the statute should be examined to determine the precise provisions. "Same sps." means that the law specifies that the spouse receives the same amount of preference as the disabled spouse. "Same fed." means that the benefit is the same as that which the federal government provides.

## (14) Provision Made for POWs Same as Disabled

The law explicitly provides that persons who were incarcerated as prisoners of war (POWs) are eligible to receive employment preference. The amount of the preference is the same as that which a disabled veteran would receive.

## (15) No Limit on Use of Preference When State Employees Not Being Considered

The law sets no limit on the number of times that a veteran can invoke the law pertaining to employment preference, as long as no other state employees are being considered for the position in question. Refer to the chapter "Overview of Federal and State Statutes," subhead "One-time Preference." Most often a veteran is allowed to invoke the law pertaining to preference only once, upon initial entry into the civil service. This is not the case in this state. A veteran can invoke the law an unlimited number of times as long as no other state employees are being considered for the job in question.

## (16) Preference Must Apply to County & City

The employment preference which is required by state law must also be given to honorably discharged veterans by the other political entities within the state, i.e., counties and cities. Barring any language in the law to the contrary, the amount of preference would presumably be the same as that which the veteran would receive from the state. Within this context, one should realize that some statutes distinguish between political entities and governmental entities. The latter are the administrative divisions within the state government such as the Division of Personnel. Accordingly, the statutes should be examined carefully in this regard.

## (17) Federal Definition of Veteran

Whatever definition the federal government uses to define the term "veteran" is required by the laws of these states.

## (18) Preference Allowed for POW Same as Regular Vet

The law provides that persons who endured incarceration as prisoners of war (POWs) will receive the same amount of employment preference as does the regular veteran (not a disabled veteran).

## (19) Pref. Allowed for Spouse/Widow Same as Regular Vet

The law provides that the spouse or surviving spouse of a veteran receives the same amount of preference as does a regular veteran (not a disabled veteran). There are several categories into which the veteran in question must fall in order for the spouse or surviving spouse to receive the preference. The law includes POWs and MIAs, for example. New Hampshire is an interesting case. That state distinguishes between (1) unremarried surviving spouses and (2) unremarried surviving spouses of qualifying veterans whose death was service-connected. The latter may receive a higher preference. Refer to the chapter "Overview of Federal and State Statutes," subhead "Eligibility of Kin."

## (20) Pref. Extended Beyond Civil Service for Licensees

These states provide that honorably discharged veterans who apply for state licenses to engage in a particular trade or profession receive some form of preference. The law applies to the examination which the individual takes for the license. This provision is in addition to that which requires employment preference.

## (21) Vet Must Be 100% Disabled for Preference

The provision applies to the spouse of the disabled veteran. In order for the spouse to receive employment preference, the veteran must be 100% disabled. Refer to the chapter "Overview of Federal and State Statutes," subheads "Eligibility of Kin" and "Preference Points."

## (22) Limit on Service Counted for Retention

The law provides that veterans who are on the payroll will receive retention preference during reductions-in-force (RIFs). However, the law limits the amount of military service which a veteran can invoke in order to claim retention rights during RIFs. Some military service is qualifying for retention purposes. This is another instance where the law should be read carefully. Refer to the chapter "Overview of Federal and State Statues," subhead "Retention Preference."

## (23) Limit on Times Vet Can Claim Preference in Same Jurisdiction

The state in question first provides that all of the political entities within the state must afford honorably discharged veterans employment preference. Refer to (16) above. The law limits the number of times that a veteran can claim preference within the same city or county.

## (24) Pref. Applies to Civil Service Entry, Not Retention

The employment preference in these states pertains only to initial entry into the civil service. It does not pertain to retention during RIFs. Refer to the chapter "Overview of Federal and State Statutes," subhead "Retention Preference." The author reiterates that when examining the statutes and reviewing the Quick Reference Guide, one should always remember that the converse of a provision in the law is usually applicable. That is, if a law fails to specify an attribute, then the converse is likely true. However, in the cases of these states the converse is immaterial. The law states explicitly that a veteran cannot invoke the preference for retention purposes during RIFs.

## (25) Pref. for Vet Less Than Honorable Conditions

The law specifies that a veteran who was released from active duty with a discharge under other than honorable conditions may apply for and receive employment preference. The law obviously does not require the preference to be given to such individuals. However, the law as written presumably provides for a procedure by which such individuals can have their cases reviewed. Presumably, if the circumstances justify the preference, one may receive it. This procedure is likely detailed in the applicable personnel regulations.

## (26) Surviving Spouse Benefit Same as Federal

Whatever the comparable federal law provides for surviving spouses is also afforded to the surviving spouses here.

## (27) Spouse of Disabled Vet Same as Federal

Whatever the comparable federal law provides for spouses is also afforded to spouses here.

## (28) % of Disability Specified

Most often this is the degree or percentage of disability which a veteran must have in order to be declared officially disabled and thereby receive the higher employment preference. However, in some states this percentage refers to the degree to which the veteran must be declared disabled in order for the spouse to receive employment preference. Refer to the chapter "Overview of Federal and State Statutes" subhead "Veteran Defined: Percentage of Disability." "Same Fed." means that the benefit is the same as that which the federal government provides.

## (29) Disabled Vet Exempt from Exam

A disabled veteran is exempt from having to take an examination for the types of positions specified.

## (30) Specify "Honorable Discharge"

These states are explicit in requiring a veteran to have an honorable discharge to receive employment preference. However, some states also qualify this language and require only that the discharge must have been under honorable conditions. The only point here is that the term "honorable discharge" is explicit in the law.

## (31) Pref. for Citizens Who Served Allied Force in War

These states require that persons who served forces which were allied to the U.S. in wartime must receive employment preference.

## (32) Preference in Public Works Projects

The law requires that persons who are employed in public works projects must receive employment preference.

## (33) Preference for Purple Heart Recipients

The law requires that recipients of the Purple Heart (P. H.) receive employment preference. This attribute is not necessarily mutually exclusive to (46) below.

## (34) Pref. Allowed for Merchant Marine Service

These states provide that persons who served in the Merchant Marine receive some form of preference. The law should be examined carefully in order to determine what periods of service are qualifying.

## (35) Pref. for Non-War Veterans & National Guard

These states allow for some form of employment preference for veterans who did not serve during specified periods of hostilities. These states further allow preference for persons who served in the National Guard during certain periods or under certain circumstances. Where there is a number, then this is the amount of the preference.

## (36) Retiree Gets Same Preference as Regular Veteran

Military retirees receive the same amount of employment preference as "regular" (not disabled) veterans. "Und-04" means that the individual must have retired at a paygrade under 0-4 in order to receive the same preference as a "regular" veteran. Conversely, all who retired as a senior officer are excluded from receiving the preference. "Except." means that this state has an exception in its statute. This exception carries the same message as those states which have the term "Und-04" in their comparable statutes.

This state merely expresses the same concept in different and unique language. As the author interprets the statute, all persons who retired at pay-grade 0-4 and above (senior officers) are excluded from receiving employment preference. Here is a classic example of a statute which should be examined carefully by the reader in order to secure the message which the legislature sought to convey, and which the reader believes was intended. Note also that this appears to be a good example in which the state laws echo the language of the comparable Federal statute.

## (37) SPOUSE LOSES PREFERENCE WHEN VETERAN RECOVERS

The law requires that the spouse of a disabled veteran receive some employment preference. However, when and if the veteran spouse recovers from the disability, then the spouse loses the preference. The applicable personnel regulation would specify the precise procedure for accomplishing this.

## (38) PREF. FOR DEPENDENT PARENT OF DISABL./DECEASED VET

The dependent parent of the disabled or deceased veteran receives this amount of preference. The law may apply to either or both, depending on the state. Note that in one state where this attribute applies, Massachusetts, the law pertains to the dependent parent of the deceased, not the disabled, veteran.

## (39) PREF. FOR SURVIVING SPOUSE OF NON-WAR DECEASED VET

The law allows for preference to be given to the surviving spouse of the veteran whose death did not necessarily result from hostilities or during a designated period of hostilities. Contrast with (2) above.

## (40) DISABLED VETS HAVE RETENTION RIGHTS OVER ALL

During reductions-in-force (RIFs), disabled veterans have retention rights over all others.

## (41) SPECIAL MEDAL RECIPIENTS EXEMPT FROM EXAM

Those veterans who are recipients of special medals such as the Congressional Medal of Honor are exempt from having to be examined for certain positions. Refer to the law to determine which medals are applicable.

## (42) Pref. in Promotional Exam for Disabled Vets

The law allows for preference for disabled veterans in promotional examinations. Refer to the chapter "Overview of Federal and State Statutes," subhead "One-time Preference." Generally, employment preferences pertain only to one's initial entry into the civil service, for which one has to take an open competitive examination. This state makes an exception for disabled veterans in promotional examinations. The number is the amount of the preference.

## (43) Pref. for Both Initial & Promotional Appointment

These states allow for preference during open competitive examinations for initial entry into the civil service. Veterans also have the added benefit of preference during promotional examinations for advancement after initial entry. Refer to the chapter "Overview of Federal and State Statutes," subhead "One-time Preference."

## (44) Preference Only for U.S. Citizen

Only persons who claim U.S. citizenship can claim the preference. Presumably a person who did serve in the Armed Forces of the United States under honorable conditions but who is not a citizen cannot claim the preference unless and until the individual is granted citizenship.

## (45) Disabled Vets Put at Top of Certificate

Disabled veterans are always placed at the top of the certificate or register, irrespective of their earned score on an examination.

## (46) Special Pref. for Purple Heart Recipient or Disabled

This state grants a special type of preference for recipients of the Purple Heart (P. H.) or for disabled veterans. This attribute is not necessarily mutually exclusive to (33) above.

## (47) Selective Service (Draftees) Eligible

Persons who were subjected to the Selective Service (draft) laws of the U.S. are eligible to receive preference. This provision apparently is in effect irrespective of the dates during which the individual served. Refer to (2) above. Those states listed for both attributes (2) and (47) also require that an individual be a war veteran. This requirement is an apparent attempt to protect individuals who were conscripted into the armed forces. One should also further realize that there are few periods during which the United States was involved in hostilities with a foreign power that the Selective Service Act was not in effect.

Refer also to (1) above. Note that every state which is marked for that attribute is also marked for (47). It is therefore implicit in the laws of the states for which (1) is marked that (47) must also apply.

## (48) DISABLED VET HAS UNLIMITED PREFERENCE

Disabled veterans are not restricted by the fifteen year time limit for applying for preference which applies to "regular" (not disabled) veterans. Note that this state has set a deadline for applying for preference. This deadline applies to veterans who served during specified periods.

## (49) SPECIAL PREFERENCE ON MUNICIPAL EXAMS

The law requires that the political entities within the state (counties, municipalities) give preference to veterans. Refer to (16) above. Municipalities are further required to give additional preference.

## (50) PREFERENCE FOR ORPHANS

The orphans of a deceased veteran are eligible for some form of preference.

## (51) CONSCIENTIOUS OBJECTORS EXCLUDED

Conscientious objectors (C.O.s) are excluded from receiving any form of preference. This pertains to the provision in the now-suspended Selective Service (draft) laws which allowed certain individuals to object to military service on moral grounds. See (47) above. Some persons were nonetheless conscripted and did serve and were discharged, possibly under honorable conditions. A celebrated Supreme Court case (403 US 698) has documented that an individual was, during the Vietnam War, ordered to report for induction into the armed forces, even though this person had previously claimed C.O. status. Theoretically this individual may have eventually been inducted despite his prior claim of C.O. status. This person may also have subsequently been discharged under honorable conditions. However, the fact that this person did previously claim C.O. status is apparent grounds for excluding such a person from receiving employment preference. The actual case was originally adjudicated in a U.S. District Court in a state which has this provision.

## (52) Disabled Pref. Over All in Non-Competitive Exam

Disabled veterans are automatically placed at the top of a register or certificate for positions for which a competitive examination is not held.

## (53) Preference Allowed for Divorced Wives

The law requires that in some cases divorced wives must receive preference if they are financially dependent upon an honorably discharged veteran.

| 1-14 | 1. Veteran | 2. War veteran | 3. Veteran only through Vietnam | 4. All vets move to top of cert | 5. All war vets move to top of cert | 6. Campaign badge needed for pref. | 7. State residency | 8. Residency required (at time of application) | 9. Prior res. req. (at time of induct.) | 10. Time limit on benefit after disch. | 11. Time limit to apply for pref. | 12. Coast Guard service included | 13. Pref. extended to spouse of disabled | 14. Provision made for POWs (same as disabled) |
|---|---|---|---|---|---|---|---|---|---|---|---|---|---|---|
| AL (5)† | X | | | | | | | | | | | X | 10 | |
| AK (5) | | X | | | | | X | | | | | | | X |
| AZ (5) | X | | | | | | | | | | | | 5 | |
| AR (10%) | X | | | | | | | | | | | | | |
| CA (10) | X | | | | | | | | | | | | 10 | |
| CO (5) | | X | | | | | X | | | | | | 5 | |
| CT (5) | | X | | | | | X | | | | | | 10 | |
| DE (5) | | X | | | | | X | X | | X | | | | |
| DC (5) | | X | | | | | X | | | 5yrs. | | | 10 | |
| FL | | X | X | | | | X | X | | | | | | |
| GA (5) | | X | | | | | X | | | | | | | |
| HI (5) | X | | | | | | | | | | | | 10 | |
| ID (5) | | X | | | | | X | X | X | | | | 10 | |
| IL (5) | | X | | | | | X | | | | | X | 10 | |
| IN (5) | | X | | | | | X | | | | | | 10 | |
| IA (5) | | X | | | | | X | X | | | | | | |
| KS (5) | | X | X | | | | X | | | | | | | |
| KY (5) | X | | | | | | | | | | | | 10 | |
| LA (5) | | X | | | | | X | | | | | | 10 | |
| ME (5) | | X | | | | | X | | | | | X | 10 | |
| MD(10) | X | | | | | | 5yrs. | | | | | | 10 | |
| MA | X | | | X | | | | | | | | | | |
| MI (5) | | X | | | | | X | 2yrs. | | 5yrs. | | | 10 | |
| MN (5) | X | | | | | | | | | | | | | |
| MS (5) | | X | | | | | X | | | | | | | |
| MO (5) | X | | | | | | | | | | | | 5 | |

†The figure in this position represents the numerical amount of preference which the laws require to be added to the passing scores of veterans' examinations.

| | 1. Veteran | 2. War veteran | 3. Veteran only through Vietnam | 4. All vets move to top of cert | 5. All war vets move to top of cert | 6. Campaign badge needed for pref. | 7. State residency | 8. Residency required (at time of application) | 9. Prior res. req. (at time of induct.) | 10. Time limit on benefit after disch. | 11. Time limit to apply for pref. | 12. Coast Guard service included | 13. Pref. extended to spouse of disabled | 14. Provision made for POWs (same as disabled) |
|---|---|---|---|---|---|---|---|---|---|---|---|---|---|---|
| MT (5)† | X | | | | | | | | | | | X | 10 | |
| NE (5) | | X | | | | X | | | | | | | | |
| NV (FIVE) | X | | | | | | SP PRO | | | | | 5 | | |
| NH | | X | | | | X | X | | | | | | 5 | |
| NJ | | X | | | X | X | | | | | | | | |
| NM (5) | X | | | | | | | | | | | | | |
| NY (5) | | X | | | | X | | | X | | | | | |
| NC (10) | | X | | | | X | | | | | | | 5 | |
| ND (5) | | X | X | | | X | X | | | | | | 10 | |
| OH (20%) | | X | | | | X | | X | | | | X | | |
| OK (5) | X | | | | | | 1yr. | | | | | | 5 | |
| OR (5) | X | X | X | | | X | | | | 15yrs. | | | | |
| PA (10) | | X | | | | X | | | | | | X | | |
| RI | | X | | | | X | | | | | | | | |
| SC (5) | X | | | | | | | | | | | X | SAME FED. | |
| SD | | X | | | | X | X | | | | | | | |
| TN (5) | | X | | | | X | X | 2yrs. | | | | | 10 | |
| TX (10) | | X | | | | X | X | 5yrs. | | | | X | * | |
| UT (5) | X | | | | | | | | | | | | SAME SPS. | |
| VT (5) | X | | | | | | | | | | | | 10 | |
| VA (5) | | | X | | | | | | | | | | | |
| WA (10) | | X | | | | X | | | | | 8yrs. | X | | |
| WV (5) | | X | | | | X | | | | | | | | |
| WI (5) | | X | | | | X | X | X | X | | | | SAME SPS. | |
| WY (5) | | X | | | | X | 1yr. | X | X | | | | SAME SPS. | |
| U.S. (5) | | X | | | | X | | | | | | X | 10 | |

†The figure in this position represents the numerical amount of preference which the laws require to be added to the passing scores of veterans' examinations.

144

# 15–27

| | 15. No limit on use of pref. when state empl. not being considered | 16. Pref. must apply to county & city | 17. Federal definition of veteran | 18. Pref. allowed for POW same as regular veteran | 19. Pref. allowed for spouse/widow same as regular veteran | 20. Pref. extended beyond civil service for licensees | 21. Vet must be 100% disabl. for pref. | 22. Limit on service counted for retention | 23. Limit on times vet can claim pref. in same jurisdiction | 24. Pref. applies to C.S. entry, not reten. | 25. Pref. for vet. less than hon. cond. | 26. Surv. spouse benefit same as fed. | 27. Spouse of disabled vet same as fed. |
|---|---|---|---|---|---|---|---|---|---|---|---|---|---|
| AL (5)† | | | | | | | | | | | | | |
| AK (5) | X | | | | | | | | | | | | |
| AZ (5) | | X | X | X | X | | | | | | | | |
| AR (10%) | | | | | | X | | | | | | | |
| CA (10) | | | | | | | X | | | | | | |
| CO (5) | | X | | | | | | X | X | | | | |
| CT (5) | | | | | | | | | | | | | |
| DE (5) | | | | | | | | | | X | | | |
| DC (5) | | | X | | | | | | | X | X | X | X |
| FL | | | | | | | | | | | | | |
| GA (5) | | X | | | | | | | | | | | |
| HI (5) | | | | | | | | | | | | | |
| ID (5) | | X | | | | | | | | | | | |
| IL (5) | | | | | | | | | | | | | |
| IN (5) | | | | | | | | | | | | | |
| IA (5) | | X | | | | | | | | X | | | |
| KS (5) | | X | | | | | | | | X | | | |
| KY (5) | | | | | | | | | | X | | | |
| LA (5) | | X | | | X | | | | | | | | |
| ME (5) | | | | | | | | | | | | | |
| MD(10) | | X | | | | | | | | | | | |
| MA | | X | | | | | | | | | | | |
| MI (5) | | X | | | | | | | | X | | | |
| MN (5) | | | | | | | | | | X | | | |
| MS (5) | | | | | | | | | | | | | |
| MO (5) | | | | | | | | | | X | | | |

†The figure in this position represents the numerical amount of preference which the laws require to be added to the passing scores of veterans' examinations.

| 15-27 | 15. No limit on use of pref. when state empl. not being considered | 16. Pref. must apply to county & city | 17. Federal definition of veteran | 18. Pref. allowed for POW same as regular veteran | 19. Pref. allowed for spouse/widow same as regular veteran | 20. Pref. extended beyond civil service for licensees | 21. Vet must be 100% disabl. for pref. | 22. Limit on service counted for retention | 23. Limit on times vet can claim pref. in same jurisdiction | 24. Pref. applies to C.S. entry, not reten. | 25. Pref. for vet. less than hon. cond. | 26. Surv. spouse benefit same as fed. | 27. Spouse of disabled vet same as fed. |
|---|---|---|---|---|---|---|---|---|---|---|---|---|---|
| MT (5)† | X | | | | | | | | | X | | | |
| NE (5) | | | | | | | | | | X | | | |
| NV (FIVE) | | X | | | | | | | | X | | | |
| NH | X | | | | | | X | | | X | | | |
| NJ | | | | | | | | | | X | | | |
| NM (5) | | | | | | | | | | X | | | |
| NY (5) | X | | | | | | | | | | | | |
| NC (10) | | | | | | | | | | | | | |
| ND (5) | X | | | | | | | | | X | | | |
| OH (20%) | X | | | | | | | | | X | | | |
| OK (5) | | | | | | | | | | | | | |
| OR (5) | | | | | | | | | | X | | | |
| PA (10) | X | | | | | | | | | X | | | |
| RI | | | | | | | | | | X | | | |
| SC (5) | | X | X | | | | | | X | | | | |
| SD | X | | | | | | | | | X | | | |
| TN (5) | | | | | | | | X | | X | | | |
| TX (10) | | X | | | | | | | | X | | | |
| UT (5) | | X | | | | | | | | X | | | |
| VT (5) | | | | | | | | | | | | | |
| VA (5) | | | | | | | | | | X | | | |
| WA (10) | | X | | | | | | | | X | | | |
| WV (5) | | | | | | | | | | X | | | |
| WI (5) | | | | | | | | | | X | | | |
| WY (5) | | X | X | | | | | | | X | | | |
| U.S. (5) | | | | | | | | | X | | | | |

†The figure in this position represents the numerical amount of preference which the laws require to be added to the passing scores of veterans' examinations.

| 28–41 | 28. % of disability specified | 29. Disabled vet exempt from exam | 30. Specify "honorable discharge" | 31. Pref. for citizens who served allied force in war | 32. Pref. in public works projects | 33. Pref. for Purple Heart recip. | 34. Pref. for merch. marine serv. | 35. Pref. for non-war vet & nat. guard | 36. Retiree gets same preference as regular vet | 37. Spouse loses pref. when vet recovers | 38. Pref. for dep. par. of disabl./dec. vet | 39. Pref. for surviving spouse of non-war deceased vet | 40. Disab. have reten. rights over all | 41. Special medal recipient exempt from exam |
|---|---|---|---|---|---|---|---|---|---|---|---|---|---|---|
| AL (5)† | | | | | | | | | | | | | | |
| AK (5) | | | | | | X | | X | | | | | | |
| AZ (5) | | | | | | | | | | | | | | |
| AR (10%) | | | X | | | | | | | | | | | |
| CA (10) | | | | | | | | | | | | | | |
| CO (5) | | | | | | | | | X | | | | | |
| CT (5) | | | | | | | | | X | | | | | |
| DE (5) | | | | | | | | | X | | | | | |
| DC (5) | 30% | | | | | | | | | | | | | |
| FL | 30% | X | | | | | | | | | | | | |
| GA (5) | 10% | | X | | | | | | | | | | | |
| HI (5) | | | | X | | X | | | X | | | X | | |
| ID (5) | | | | | | | | | X | | | X | | |
| IL (5) | | | | X | X | X | X | 3 | X | | X | X | | |
| IN (5) | 10% | | | | | | | 2 | X | | | X | | |
| IA (5) | | | X | | X | X | | | X | | | | | |
| KS (5) | 10% | | | | X | | | | X | | | | | |
| KY (5) | | | | | | | | X | X | X | 10 | 10 | | |
| LA (5) | | | | | | | | | X | | 10 | | | |
| ME (5) | 10% | | | | | | | | | | 10 | 5 | | |
| MD(10) | | | X | | | | | | | | | 10 | | |
| MA | | | | X | | | | | | | X | | X | X |
| MI (5) | 50% | | | X | | | | | | | | 5 | | |
| MN (5) | | | | | | | | | | | | | | |
| MS (5) | | | X | | | | | | X | | | | | |
| MO (5) | 30% | | | | | | | | | | | | | |

†The figure in this position represents the numerical amount of preference which the laws require to be added to the passing scores of veterans' examinations.

| 28-41 | 28. % of disability specified | 29. Disabled vet exempt from exam | 30. Specify "honorable discharge" | 31. Pref. for citizens who served allied force in war | 32. Pref. in public works projects | 33. Pref. for Purple Heart recip. | 34. Pref. for merch. marine serv. | 35. Pref. for non-war vet & nat. guard | 36. Retiree gets same preference as regular vet | 37. Spouse loses pref. when vet recovers | 38. Pref. for dep. par. of disabl./dec. vet | 39. Pref. for surviving spouse of non-war deceased vet | 40. Disab. have reten. rights over all | 41. Special medal recipient exempt from exam |
|---|---|---|---|---|---|---|---|---|---|---|---|---|---|---|
| MT (5)† | | | | | | X | X | | | | 10 | | | |
| NE (5) | | | | | | | | | X | | | | | |
| NV (FIVE) | | | | | | | | | X | | | | | |
| NH | | | | | X | | | | X | | | | | |
| NJ | | | X | | | | | | X | | | | | |
| NM (5) | | | | | | | | | X | | | | | |
| NY (5) | 10% | | | | | | | | | | | | | |
| NC (10) | | | | | | | | | X | | | | | |
| ND (5) | | | | | | | | | X | | | | | |
| OH (20%) | | | | | | | | | X | | | | | |
| OK (5) | 30% | | | | | | | | X | | | | | |
| OR (5) | | | | | | X | | | | | | | | |
| PA (10) | | | X | | | | | | X | | | | | |
| RI | | | | | X | | X | | X | X | | | | |
| SC (5) | SAME FED. | | | | X | X | | | UND. 0-4 | X | X | X | | |
| SD | | | X | X | | | | | X | | | | | |
| TN (5) | 100% | | | | | | | | X | | | | | |
| TX (10) | | | | | X | | | | | | | | | |
| UT (5) | any% | | | | 10 | | | | UND. 0-4 | | | X | | |
| VT (5) | | | X | | | | | | EXCEPT. | | | | | |
| VA (5) | | | X | | | | | | X | | | | | |
| WA (10) | | | X | | | | | | | | | | | |
| WV (5) | | | | | | X | | | X | | | | | |
| WI (5) | | | | | | | | | X | | X | | | |
| WY (5) | 10% | | | | X | | | | X | | | | | |
| U.S. (5) | 10% | | | | | X | | | UND. 0-4 | X | X | X | | |

†The figure in this position represents the numerical amount of preference which the laws require to be added to the passing scores of veterans' examinations.

| 42-53 | 42. Pref. in prom. exam for disabled | 43. Pref. for both initial & promotional appointment | 44. Pref. only for U.S. citizen | 45. Disabled vets put at top of cert. | 46. Spec. pref. for P.H. rec. or disabled | 47. Selective service (draftees) eligible | 48. Disabled vet has unlimited pref. | 49. Spec. pref. on municipal exam | 50. Preference for orphans | 51. C.O.s excluded | 52. Disabled have pref. over all in non-competitive exam | 53. Pref. for divorced wives |
|---|---|---|---|---|---|---|---|---|---|---|---|---|
| AL (5)† | | | | | | | | | | | | |
| AK (5) | | | | | | | | | | | | |
| AZ (5) | | | | | | | | | | | | |
| AR (10%) | | | | | | | | | | | | |
| CA (10) | | | | | | | | | | | | |
| CO (5) | | | | | | | | | | | | |
| CT (5) | | | | | | | | | | | | |
| DE (5) | | | | | | | | | | | | |
| DC (5) | | | | | | | | | | | | |
| FL | | | | | | | | | | | | |
| GA (5) | | | | | | | | | | | | |
| HI (5) | | | | | | | | | | | | |
| ID (5) | | | | X | | | | | | | | |
| IL (5) | | | | | | X | | | | | | |
| IN (5) | | | | | | X | | | | | | |
| IA (5) | | | | | X | | X | | | | | |
| KS (5) | | | | | | | | | | X | | |
| KY (5) | | | | | | X | | | | | | |
| LA (5) | | | | | | | | | | | | |
| ME (5) | X | | | X | | | | | | | | |
| MD(10) | | | | | | | | | | | | |
| MA | | | | | | | | | | | | |
| MI (5) | | | | | | X | | | | | | |
| MN (5) | 5 | | | | X | | | | | | | |
| MS (5) | | X | | | | | | | | | | |
| MO (5) | | | | | | | | | | | | |

†The figure in this position represents the numerical amount of preference which the laws require to be added to the passing scores of veterans' examinations.

| | 42. Pref. in prom. exam for disabled | 43. Pref. for both initial & promotional appointment | 44. Pref. only for U.S. citizen | 45. Disabled vets put at top of cert. | 46. Spec. pref. for P.H. rec. or disabled | 47. Selective service (draftees) eligible | 48. Disabled vet has unlimited pref. | 49. Spec. pref. on municipal exam | 50. Preference for orphans | 51. C.O.s excluded | 52. Disabled have pref. over all in non-competitive exam | 53. Pref. for divorced wives |
|---|---|---|---|---|---|---|---|---|---|---|---|---|
| MT (5)† | | | X | | | | | | | | | |
| NE (5) | | | | | | | | | | | | |
| NV (FIVE) | | X | | | | X | | | | | | |
| NH | | | | | | | | | | | | |
| NJ | | | | X | | | | | | | | |
| NM (5) | | | | | | | | | | | | |
| NY (5) | X | X | X | | | | | | | | | |
| NC (10) | | | | | | X | | | | | | |
| ND (5) | | | | X | X | | | | | | | |
| OH (20%) | | | | X | | X | | | | | | |
| OK (5) | | | | | X | X | X | | | | | |
| OR (5) | | | | | | | X | | | | | |
| PA (10) | | X | | | | | | X | | | | |
| RI | | | | | | | | | | | | |
| SC (5) | | | | | | X | | | | | | |
| SD | | X | X | | | X | | | | | | |
| TN (5) | | | | | | | | | | | | |
| TX (10) | | | | | | | | | X | X | X | |
| UT (5) | | | | | | X | | | | | | |
| VT (5) | | LAW UNCL | | | | X | | | | | | |
| VA (5) | | | | | | | | | | | | |
| WA (10) | | | | | | | | | | | | |
| WV (5) | | | | | | | | | | | | |
| WI (5) | | | | | | X | | | | | | X |
| WY (5) | | | | | | | | | | | | |
| U.S. (5) | | | | | | X | | | | | | |

†The figure in this position represents the numerical amount of preference which the laws require to be added to the passing scores of veterans' examinations.

150

# BIBLIOGRAPHY

Berko, Robert L. *Complete Guide to Federal and State Benefits for Veterans, Their Families and Survivors: How to Get All the Benefits You Are Entitled to Under the Latest Laws.* 12th ed. South Orange NJ: Consumer Education Research Center, 1994.

Coffelt, Louis D. *A Guide to Veterans' Affairs Law and Practice.* 1st ed. Arlington VA: Dewey Publications, 1990.

United States. Department of Veterans Affairs. *Federal Benefits for Veterans and Dependents.* Washington DC: U. S. Government Printing Office, 1998.

United States. House of Representatives. Committee on Veterans Affairs. *State Veterans' Laws: Digests of State Laws Regarding Rights, Benefits and Privileges of Veterans and Their Dependents.* Washington, DC: U. S. Government Printing Office, 1992.

# INDEX